SPEAK
with
NO FEAR

Go from a nervous, nauseated, and
sweaty speaker to an excited, energized, and
passionate presenter

Mike Acker

https://www.stepstoadvance.com
To contact, please e-mail: contact@stepstoadvance.com

READ FIRST

Thank you for investing in my book.

As an appreciation, I'd love to give you a free gift.

THE 3 QUESTIONS & THE 3 CLASSICS

This is the lesson I start out with
when coaching speech clients.

This lesson has helped hundreds of people
gain clarity and direction in creating their speech.

Visit this link or use the QR code for your free gift:
https://3and3.stepstoadvance.com/book

ACKNOWLEDGEMENTS

I'd like to thank three sets of people: my clients, my family, and our friends.

I'm honored to coach people in their leadership, career, and life. As I work to help you get better, you make me better. Thank you for allowing me to speak into your life to improve your skills and help direct you on your path.

My wife, Taylor, and our son, Paxton, allowed me the time to get away each morning to put years of lessons onto electronic paper. I was often interrupted (in a good way) with coffee, hugs, and with my little guy wanting to sit on my lap as I typed this out early in the morning. I love you both!

To our friends – thank you! We love the groups we have been part of over the years. You mean so much to us. Thank you for being more than friends. You have been family, supporters, and cheerleaders. Here's to many more years together!

"Courage is not the absence of fear, but the mastery of it."

Mark Twain

Contents

INTRODUCTION:
YOU ARE NOT ALONE

I was in the 7th grade. Pimples, growth spurts, and a cracking voice defined my exterior. My parents had forced me to go to a new school in a different country. I was an outsider to the school and a foreigner to the nation of Mexico where my family had transplanted.

The day came when I had to give my first presentation. La Maestra (the teacher) called me forward. All eyes rested on me. Insecurity, doubt, and fear marked my interior. My nerves fried as I stood to speak to the class of forty peers. As my presentation began, so did the laughter. Forty teenagers cackled at me as I stood all—alone. I sped through my words, turning the presentation from merely okay to unintelligible.

Finally, it was over. I made it through the rest of the day amidst teasing and others talking about me behind my back. I literally ran home (we lived 3 blocks away).

Fear gripped me, causing psychosomatic sickness to set in the next day so that I could skip school. I didn't ever want to do that again.

YOU DON'T HAVE TO BE AFRAID

Fear is why you bought this book. My guess is that you have an upcoming event at which to speak. Or your job or schooling requires you to get in front of people constantly. Each time this happens, your stomach drops, you begin to sweat, and you want to throw up.

I get it.

You don't have to be afraid any longer. This book can help you. You will learn 7 strategies you can begin today. These strategies will give you a new perspective, they will prepare you, and they will give you actions to practice. As you implement these strategies, your fear will begin to fade.

How do I know that? I have personally acted out these strategies. Years later, I am widely educated and I am broadly experienced in communication. Additionally, I started a company called ADVANCE and I have twenty clients work with me each week to grow their skills. They are in the middle of conquering fear, or have already learned to conquer their fear. You can do this too!

I understand what you're feeling right now, and I promise you, I know how to get you where you want to go. You can overcome your fear.

I know what it's like to be nervous, worried, sweaty, and anxious. You are not alone. Today, you can take a step in a new direction. You can begin the journey to overcome your fear *right now*. If you are overwhelmed by the fear of speaking, begin to believe that things are going to start to change today. You don't have to be afraid forever.

Or maybe you're a student of communication, and you just want to hone your skills. You already know how to conquer your fear; you just want to get better at controlling your anxiety and your nerves. This book will help you develop that ability.

Or maybe it's just been a while since you've spoken in front of people, and you want to regain a sense of mastery.

Each week, I work with all kinds of clients who express the desire to get better. I believe you are committed to improving as well, and I applaud you as you take this next step. These 7 strategies can be added to your tool belt if you are brand-new or just need to sharpen the tools that you already have.

Ultimately, this book will help you. You can take these 7 strategies and immediately get to work to overcome your fear. If you want to skip ahead, just go to https://subscribe. stepstoadvance.com/action to download my action checklist. These will give you specific actions to practice. However, this entire book will do more than just provide actions to take: it will give you the understanding to help you develop a new mindset.

Whatever your situation currently is, I understand. I used to get sweaty, nervous, and nauseated even to small groups. Now, I have had the chance to speak to 3,000 people at civic engagements, lead leadership workshops, speak to several thousand people at a megachurch, engage audiences of kids and youth, speak at churches of many sizes, and many more events.

MY PROMISE TO YOU

I promise you that you can do this. You can speak with no fear.

Where you are is *not* where you have to be.

Don't wait any longer. One day turns into one week. One week turns into a month, into a year, into a decade, and into a lifetime. Don't let life pass you by while you wrestle with the same old enemy of fear. Do something about it.

Take action today. Begin to read. Begin to learn these strategies. Start now.

"Now is the time to fix the next 10 years."

Jim Rohn

THE SEVEN STRATEGIES

1. Uncover & Clean the Wound

2. Imagine the Worst

3. You Be You

4. Speak to One

5. It's Not About You

6. Channel The Power

7. Be in the Moment

"We are what we believe we are."

C.S. Lewis

BEFORE YOU BEGIN:
BELIEVE

You are welcome to jump into the strategies below. I won't stop you from taking action. Just promise me that you won't start with doubt.

Doubt deters you from taking strategies seriously. Doubt erodes confidence. Doubt makes truth seem like lies. Doubt will feed your fear and give you more speaking nightmares. So you have to let go of your doubts and start believing in yourself.

Where you are is *not* where you have to be.

This sentence was included in my introduction. Do you believe it? Do you believe in yourself? At least some part of you does. Otherwise you wouldn't have picked up this book! Let's build on this belief. Take a moment and whisper the immortal words from the classic story, *The Little Engine That Could*, "I think I can. I think I can. I think I can."

Are you struggling? Do you find yourself dwelling on negative thoughts? "It's not going to work for me." "I'm just not a good speaker." "I'm an introvert. I just can't." "I've tried in the past, and it didn't work."

If you are struggling to believe, will you suspend disbelief while you read?

Read this book as a believer, not as a skeptic. Education will often teach you to think critically. Keep that mindset for work and academics. This book needs you to think receptively. Trade in any negativity for positivity. Think well of yourself. Believe in yourself. Where you are is *not* where you have to be.

I have lived this mantra. I really can help you live it as well. That is why I started my coaching practice, ADVANCE, Coaching and Consulting (https://www.stepstoadvance.com). I help people take their next step forward so they can advance their goals, business, skill sets, careers, and life. I want to help you. And *belief* is where that help begins.

I believe in you. You can turn your speaking nightmares into living your dreams.

MY SPEAKING NIGHTMARES

Imagine (or better yet, recall) one of these scenarios: You are asked to give a toast for a wedding. You are requested to give a presentation on your area of expertise. Your company has grown and you want to pitch an idea to obtain additional capital. You need to give some kind of speech or presentation. And what happens? You're nervous. Sweat starts to pool under your arms. Butterflies begin to flutter in your abdomen. You want to throw up. Your anxiety causes you to endlessly ramble. You wish you could quit the speech and run away. But you can't; you have to get up in front of people and speak.

If you have a speech coming up, then you are being forced to face the number-one fear in America (above even death). Yes, you read that right; public speaking is often ranked as the number-one fear in America. Do you relate? You would rather die than speak in front of people!

If you feel fear, anxiety, and nervousness at the prospect of public speaking, then you are not alone. Hundreds, thousands, actually millions of people are right there with you. And each day I get to help some of them overcome that fear.

You don't have to have that same fear forever.

You really don't. I believe in you. You *can* conquer that fear!

I can help you. I can't erase the fear but I can give you understanding, tips, and skills that will ease your fear. That fear can devolve into the appropriate type of energy. I can teach you how. It's what I do.

Don't wait to get started. Don't push this off to another day. Today is the day! Don't delay. Unattended fear only feeds on itself and grows into nightmares.

Every time I spoke in front of my middle school and high school class, I was made fun of. It became a common theme for people to laugh at my stage presence. Each month, I had to wrestle that familiar sensation that struck me when yet another presentation was assigned to our class. I grew friendly with the fear of public speaking. Over time, I learned how to manage the fear, but every presentation was still accompanied by fear.

Outside of my school fear, I had the opportunity during high school to speak at a banquet. I had some good thoughts to share but when I spoke it came across poorly. While I meant to honor another person, my speech seemed to focus only on myself. Later, my mom pulled me aside and rebuked me. She was embarrassed that I had talked so highly of myself. But I didn't mean to brag! I was honoring someone else. However, my speech went wrong and I was humiliated. 20+ years later, I'm still embarrassed of that speech.

These negative experiences tainted me. After the banquet, I panicked at the next opportunity to speak in front of others. "What if I screw up again? What if I embarrass myself? What will my mom think? I should just shut up. I should run away. I should fake sickness. I should move to Australia. I should become a silent monk. Yes, I will become a monk." And that is what I did. I moved to Australia and became a monk. I don't have to speak to people anymore...

Of course not. That isn't how life works. You can't run from public speaking. At some point in your life, you will have to speak at your business, your school, a wedding, a memorial, a party, an interview, or one of a hundred different scenarios. You will have to get up in front of people, so you might as well learn how to do without fear. And that is what I did. I gradually worked on managing my emotions. I learned how to use my personality, how to switch my focus, and how to use fear for good. I began to believe in myself.

I internalized how to ease my fear and turn the negative to something positive. My only wish? I wish I'd started earlier. Don't delay it anymore. Begin to believe in yourself today.

GARY'S BELIEF CHANGED MY LIFE

In college, I took my first class on public speaking, a small class at my small private university. I stood there in front of people with the battling emotions of fear and excitement (two sides of the same coin). My abilities had grown since high school, which alleviated some of my fear. At the same time, I had failed in front of other audiences, which made me relive moments of panic.

When I gave my speech to the class, I didn't die of a heart attack, but I didn't inspire my audience, either. I guess my battling emotions agreed to call it a tie.

After the speech, the professor invited me to join the college debate team. I told him no. For a few months, he persisted. He believed that if I pushed past my insecurities, weaknesses, and fears, I could do well. He believed in me. He had coached hundreds of people to overcome their fear. He had helped hundreds of people develop the skill of public speaking so that they could attain a higher level of excellence in their career. He impressed upon me the importance of learning how to speak in front of others.

Let me do that for you. You can push past your insecurities. Your past failures don't have to mark your present reality. Your weaknesses don't have to define your work. Your fear can be relieved. As Gary believed in me, I believe in you.

As you develop this skill of public speaking, you will do better in your career. Don't miss the value of improving your speaking skills. The famed investor, Warren Buffet, attributes part of his success to taking speaking lessons as a young man. The better you speak, the better you will do. The small actions you take here will translate to great actions out there in your world.

Professor Gary Gillespie convinced me that if I joined his traveling debate and speech team, he could do something great for me. He promised me that I didn't have to remain a novice. He told me that he wanted me on his team.

(Later, I realized that the incredible senior class was graduating and the debate team was in desperate need of new members, but I didn't know it at the time!)

Finally, I believed him. I started imagining myself not to be a bad speaker, or just an okay speaker, or just a good speaker. I believed I could be great.

You don't have to be the same nervous speaker you are today. You don't have to be afraid. You don't have to be insecure. You can become great.

"Mike, I'm skipping to the actions."

Don't skip ahead. The most important action to overcome fear is to believe. Reading this book will help you believe in yourself and believe in your ability to overcome your anxiety, nerves, and dread.

BELIEVE YOU CAN

Did you see *Indiana Jones and the Raiders of the Lost Arc*? In one scene, the actor Harrison Ford must cross a deep chasm with a pit below. If he turns around, he will forfeit everything. Compelled by a deeper understanding, he puts one foot over the chasm, believing that somehow he will be able to walk across. As he steps out in belief, his foot lands on an invisible yet solid bridge. His faith allows him to move forward.

Step out in courage. Believe in a deeper understanding. You can do this. You *will* do this. And each time you do this, you will get better.

I guarantee you that if I were to speak to you face-to-face, or if you were in one of my seminars, I would look you in the eye and say, "You can do this."

Remember Mark Twain's words: "Courage is not the absence of fear, but the mastery of it."

FROM TEENAGER TO ORATOR

On September 23rd, 2016, tragedy forced together our community in Skagit County. A shooter entered the local mall less than a mile from our home. He killed five people. The community reeled in shock and quickly rallied to support each other. Three days later, we had organized a vigil outside of where the violent act had occurred. I worked with the Mayor, a well-known pastor, the police chief, and other community leaders to prepare to bring peace back to our towns which fear had stolen away.

Word of the vigil got out. Our event on September 26, Light up the Boulevard, welcomed hundreds and hundreds of people. The team of volunteers extended the blockades to hold the growing audience. People brought candles of all shapes and sizes. The police chief was speaking to two other chiefs from neighboring towns.

He beckoned me over and said, "I've never seen something like this here in Skagit county."

"How many people are here?" I inquired curiously. The lights had faded. It was impossible to count. Even the pictures failed to capture the people who crammed into the cordoned parking lot.

The three chiefs looked at each other and sized up the space. "At least 3,000."

At least 3,000.

Almost 20 years earlier, teenagers had mercilessly teased me when I stood to speak to them. Now, I was about to walk onto a stage to speak about hope to more than 3,000 people.

The moment came for my presentation. The stage called me forward. All eyes were on me. Insecurity, doubt, and fear no longer marked my interior. My nerves ignited into energy as I stood to speak to the audience of 3,000 neighbors. As my presentation began, so did the nodding. 3,000 people stood holding their candles, listening to my words in agreement with me. I was not alone. I didn't have to rush; instead I confidently took time with my words. The presentation took people from feelings of darkness to anticipation of light.

Your journey can mirror mine. You don't have to be afraid any longer. This is what life can look like. Begin to believe this truth. You can learn to enjoy presenting, selling, educating, storytelling, and speaking in public. The same strategies I used in my life, you can use in yours.

These strategies are not miraculous, but they are miracle workers. If you take action and do the assignments, you will experience results. If you take heart and believe in yourself, you will see how the work you do becomes the miracle you hope to see.

If you change your perspective, invest in your preparation, and take time to practice, then I promise you, you will overcome your fear of public speaking.

"The unexamined life is not worth living."

Socrates

UNCOVER & CLEAN THE WOUND

I've coached hundreds of people over the last 18 years of my diverse career. Most people (not all) have a reason why public speaking makes them nervous.

Most people have a story. Here is the continuation of mine.

While starting out in college, I learned about a pressing need in Seattle, which was 15 minutes away from where I attended a small university. I did my research and brought the matter to the president of the university. One-on-one I was very compelling; we could bring financial aid and manpower to an urgent homelessness issue by partnering with the local shelters. The president of the university invited me to give a short speech to the school. (This was before I joined the college's nationally ranked debate team.)

When I was asked to speak, I was excited to share my passion project, even while I was fearful of the prospect of standing under the scrutiny of a few hundred peers.

What do *you* feel when you are invited to speak for an event or on a topic that excites you? Perhaps it is a toast for a wedding. Or your business wants to implement your idea! Or your employee has been with you for 20 years and you want to honor them in front of the whole company. Maybe your project gets noticed and you have the chance to speak to an entire university.

Through my years of coaching clients in public speaking, each of these scenarios has emerged. Eduardo wanted to give an incredible toast as a groomsman, but he was nervous and disorganized. Matthew's boss wanted to hear more about his proposal for the company. Jonathan's employee had been with him for so long that he just had to do something to recognize her contribution. Fara's inspiring product landed her the chance to speak to hundreds of people at a prestigious university.

These are real people who had a real fear for a real reason. Each of them had a story. What is your story? Why are you reading this? You may be tempted to skip this part. I would. I would want to jump ahead to some 'hands-on' strategies that I could really act on. But if I did that, I would put a band-aid on a wound carrying infection on the inside.

SCRAPES, CUTS AND CAREFUL MOMS

As a kid, I played hard. It was common for me to get cuts on my knees, get back up, and play harder. I was a daredevil. I was an explorer. I was crazy.

Each time I injured myself, my Mom would eventually see me poking my knee, elbow, or another area in pain. Her questions would lead to exposing my wound. "Mike! This is infected!" I don't know how many times I heard that growing up. Too many! My mom would jump up and get the first aid kit. She would drag me to the bathroom and painfully clean my cut. She was merciless. She insisted on rubbing out all the dirt and sterilizing my cut. At times, she scrubbed while scolding me of the dangers of rusty metal or filthy streets. Only after she probed my pain did she apply Neosporin and band-aids.

You would think I would learn, but I didn't. I just kept injuring myself and kept trying to move past it.

Many people ignore their pain and run from their hurt. I see it again and again. People walk around with barely disguised limps, bandages bleeding through, or makeup to cover infections. Some are hurt so badly that their wounds cause them to react hysterically if you get near. This book is not a counseling session for relationships, failures, and anxiety. Otherwise, we would go deep into this issue over the course of several hundred pages. Please, realize this kind of behavior is not healthy. If you constantly react negatively or run from people, go to a person like my mom. Go to someone who will uncover your wound, probe your pain, and get the toxins out. Visit a counselor, join a grief group, engage in purposeful journaling, or find a great church. Don't walk around wounded. You matter too much.

Just as we cover up emotional wounds, we cover up past public speaking wounds.

MY SPEAKING WOUND

This book contains seven strategies that I now teach in Lesson One of my speech program. The following story happened before I knew any of them. Nowadays, my speech program contains 15 modules I implement with clients to improve public speaking. This story happened when these were unknown and unused. As a result, my speech was terrible.

When the president of my university invited me to speak, I felt nervous. I was excited and terrified. Yes, I lean toward being an extrovert (not as much as most people assume.) I even had some minor public speaking experience. This time, the event was bigger as several hundred of my peers gathered in the same room (many cute girls too!)

My nerves increased the moment the president invited me to the platform. I jumped up and rushed to the podium. I just knew that hundreds of the worst people in the world wanted to mock me. I started talking, but I got lost in my handwritten notes. In my confusion, I added words to make it better. Hasty improvisation turned to rambling paragraphs. I swear that the room got darker while the light on me got brighter. I started to sweat. I spoke faster. Everything in me screamed, "I just want to be done."

Fear had enveloped me.

The president of the college laid a gentle hand on my shoulder. I looked over with a startled expression. He smiled kindly as he interrupted, "Thank you, Mike, for sharing with us." Embarrassment mingled with relief as I realized he was cutting my speech short. I had blown it, and he knew it. I begrudgingly embraced the interruption as an opportunity to escape the stage and rush out of the public view. The president paraphrased my points and invited people to get involved.

I never wanted to do that again.

Is that how you feel? What is your story?

Regularly, I hear of high school presentations going the wrong way, or kids getting put on the spot by parents, or a sales pitch gone awry, or peers giving their friend a hard time. It's amazing how certain bad experiences will etch their way into our minds and stay there on a subconscious level.

Return to my wound analogy. No matter how much you cover an infected wound with bandages, clothes, or makeup, the wound will still be there. To effectively move past a wound, you need to clean it first.

WILLIAM OVERCAME HIS FEAR. YOU CAN TOO.

Uncovering and cleaning your wound is a proven strategy. This strategy works when you work it. William discovered amazing results from healing his past speaking hurts. As we worked together, I probed his fear of presenting. At a young age, he had a negative experience in front of his elementary school, leaving him extremely embarrassed and in tears. He stood in front of his friends and classmates to do a short presentation. He began to speak, but he stumbled and stuttered with his words. Embarrassment washed over him, flushing his face bright red. He rambled as he tried to make sense of what he was saying. Unlike my university president, his teacher didn't jump in to save him. He began to talk even faster, and his class began to laugh. Sweat beaded together on his forehead and dampened his palms. Shock, terror, and fear took hold of William. Finally, his teacher excused him.

His experience traumatized him. William surprised himself as he self-discovered this childhood experience had grown to influence his current anxiety when he stood in front of crowds. We probed the pain, re-examined the circumstances, and now he is armed with awareness that combats his anxiety.

William's past pain no longer defines him subconsciously.

When your past pain no longer defines *you*, then your present fear begins to be eased.

Many of my clients have experienced freedom from fear by uncovering and cleaning their wounds. Other clients dismissed it, only to later tell me that they had chosen to start journaling or see a counselor. As they took action, they too experienced freedom.

QUESTIONS TO UNCOVER YOUR WOUND

Before you continue with the other six strategies, take a moment to uncover your wound. Use these questions to reveal the source of your nervousness:

- Have you been embarrassed in front of people? What happened?

- Did you ever get put on the spot without being ready for it? How did it turn out?

- Do you have memories of multiple people making fun of you?

- Where have you fallen short of your own expectations for yourself?

- Why do you care so much about what people might think of you?

- What is the most humiliating moment in your life? (It probably had to do with people's attention being brought to a mistake you made, a failure you had, or a weakness you are insecure about.)

What causes are at the root of your fear? These questions are repeated below in the ACTION section. Use these questions to dive in and pull out insecurity, lack of preparation, unkind words, humiliating moments, and anything else that is there.

This is the beginning of the first strategy. Uncover the wound. If you don't, then every bad experience will compound, causing the weight of your fear to increase. Meanwhile, every successful experience will seemingly cause you to forget the pain. Your successes will lead you to *think* that the wound no longer exists. Ignoring your pain is the equivalent to layers of expensive, nice clothes hiding the wound from sight. The problem is that when the wound gets bumped, then the blood and pus will ooze out.

Remember the cuts on my elbows that I hid from my mom? Occasionally, I would get dressed with a button-up shirt and a nice jacket. The clothes hid the cut only until my elbow painfully bumped something hard. Because I didn't deal with my wound, it ruined my outfit.

Don't ruin future successes by ignoring past pain.

Deal with the wound. Here comes my mom to clean it out.

SCARS ARE COOL.
INFECTED SCABS ARE NOT.

I have lots of scars from my childhood. I have an inch-wide circular scar on my ankle from where the fin of a surfboard carved away a pocket of my flesh. The gash hurt at the time. Hah! What an understatement! I panicked and freaked out at the sight of blood mingling with sand and salt water. My grandpa ran to pick me up as he saw me shrieking, and we rushed to the hospital. The doctors painfully washed the sand out of the inside of my foot. Sanitizing the wound disgusted me, even though I kept watching.

The doctors did a great job uncovering and treating my wound. Because they cleaned the deep cut, there was no infection. The wound scabbed over in a healthy manner. It itched, but it did not throb. Today, it is a cool scar with a fun story to tell. Ancient scars become painless memories when the past has been healed. You can tell the story without negative emotions surrounding it.

How do you turn your nasty cut into cool scar? Uncovering the wound is not enough. "Look at the painful, disgusting cut!

Wow! That really is bad!" No. You must go beyond uncovering. Choose to clean it out.

How do you clean a speaking wound? Learn to repurpose the pain. Look through the bad and find the good therein.

- What was the outcome of your speaking wound?

- Did anything good come from your bad experience?

- Does your negative experience define you as a person?

- Picture your current self in the audience. What would you say to the past version of yourself?

- Does the memory hurt less?

My wife and I experienced four years of infertility. We desperately wanted to have kids. We discovered that conception was going to be very difficult for us. Even though we realized this was the case, we kept responding to inquiries from friends by saying we weren't ready, or we wanted to have some fun traveling first, or other fallacies. We were just covering the wound. Finally, we could cover it no longer. The doctor told us the truth and uncovered our barely-disguised wound. Hearing the truth from the doctor pained us and relieved us at the same time.

We chose to no longer pretend that everything was okay. We told friends. We cried. We shared our feelings. We began to clean out the wound by exposing our hurt to healing conversations.

After spending lots of money and experiencing the emotional roller coaster of clinical treatments, we had our first son! He is almost four now. We are back in the clinic. Infertility is a painful wound, but we keep it clean. We have discovered that through our transparency and vulnerability, we have created some incredible friendships. We have given hope to others. We have inspired family, friends, and large groups of people.

We have found the good in the bad.

Uncover the wound. Don't pretend it isn't there. Go back to revisit and relive the embarrassment, shame, failure, and fear.

Now, get in there and clean it out. Take out the bad and find the good.

As you uncover the wound to clean it out, you will watch the painful cut turn to a clean scab and, eventually, a cool scar.

ACTION:
COUNSEL YOURSELF

Take action to get healthy. What does this look like? I suggest that you take one of the following 3 actions:

1. Journal your pain.

2. Go to a counselor.

3. Turn your story into a speech.

ONE: JOURNAL YOUR PAIN.

In my twenties, hidden wounds from my teenage years surfaced. A wise woman counseled me to write about my negative experiences. She said it would help me deal with the upheaval I had undergone. Initially, I scoffed. Afterall, it wasn't *that* big of a deal and I didn't have *that* much to write about.

Skeptically, I sat down at a cafe and started typing. 3 hours later, I had cried, almost cussed out loud, and eventually experienced peace. I had delved into my pain and cleaned out toxins by writing a 5-page history of what happened. Yes, that is on the extreme side of it. Perhaps you will need to write a single paragraph, maybe a page, or – like me – you will complete 5 pages. Here lies the key to healing: relive the feelings that lead to your fear.

Use these questions to uncover the wound:

- Have you been embarrassed in front of people? What happened?

- Did you ever get put on the spot without being ready for it? How did it turn out?

- Do you have memories of multiple people making fun of you?

- Where have you fallen short of your own expectations for yourself?

- Why do you care so much about what people might think of you?

- What is the most humiliating moment in your life?

TWO: GO TO A COUNSELOR.

If the pain is deep, go to a counselor, or a group where you can discuss what happened.

I had to do that in some areas in my life, since I was harassed, bullied, and beaten while in the 9th grade. The words and actions of a few people left a mark on me that I hid for many years. Thankfully, I eventually went to a counselor and unpacked the dirty baggage I was carrying. Although my experience did not regard public speaking, it did help me accept myself, which led to increased confidence.

THREE: TURN YOUR STORY INTO A SPEECH.

Turn your story into a speech. Then deliver it to yourself, maybe to some friends, or perhaps to a larger group. This action combines uncovering and cleaning the wound along with working on a speech. You will need to uncover the wound to begin writing, but the process of writing becomes a salve as you discover what lessons you learned.

Use a simple speech structure, such as: Intro, 3 points, and conclusion.

The introduction sets the stage for 3 incidents which are at the root of your fear of speaking. The 3 points are 3 stories that happened to you and how you felt. The conclusion is how you are going to move on and not let the past define your future.

The ending of the speech becomes the lesson you want to bestow on others.

COUNSEL YOURSELF TO HEALTH

If the wound is deep, then keep working on one or more of these methods to uncover it and clean it. Fully expose it to the light. For example, if you had parents who belittled you and told you that you were worthless, and if they made fun of your childhood performances, then your current fear of public speaking is quite deep. It will take a while to unpack it.

Regardless of how deep or shallow the wound is, take action to uncover it and clean it.

"One thing that makes it possible to be an optimist is if you have a contingency plan for when all hell breaks loose."

Randy Pausch

STRATEGY #2:
IMAGINE THE WORST

Do you want to hear about the time I referred to a woman in the audience as old?

In 2006, a great church in Stanwood, Washington asked me to be their pastor. I was honored, but I also didn't know what I was doing. Public speaking had become a significant part of my life, but the audience had always comprised kids and teenagers. Now, I was speaking to a church filled with professionals: teachers, doctors, business owners, and other *real* adults.

One Sunday, I told a story about how about our guest speaker the week before had mistaken a lady in our church for my wife… yes, a very stupid story to bring up in a sermon. But that wasn't the worst part. Offhandedly, I remarked, "Because I totally go for women twice my age."

Gasp.

The audience paused and reacted appropriately. I had just branded a wonderful woman (who was just shy of 50) as old. Blood rushed into my face. Red as a tomato, I finally moved my stuttering lips and tried to clean up my mistake. Eventually, her stoic husband kindly waved his hand in the air and said, "Just move on, Mike."

I didn't live that one down for a decade. That's not it, though:

I once taught at a camp for 90 minutes, not realizing that people were bored.

I once led a symposium and put some of the people to sleep.

I once told high schoolers that we were going to be looking at pornography while I pointed at the screen. (I meant to say we were going to be discussing the effects of pornography, not looking at it!)

I once accidentally cussed in an Easter sermon.

I once spoke to a school in India in extremely fast and unintelligible English.

I once got so frustrated in a debate that I essentially yelled at the opponents.

I once told a relationship workshop that a prostitute didn't have anything to teach me.

Over the years, I have offended people, used the wrong word, left out context, forgotten my place in my notes, used "uh" far too many times, rapidly paced the stage, and performed hundreds of other mistakes.

You will too.

"Mike! What are you doing? I'm reading this and thinking about my upcoming speech, and now I'm more nervous than ever."

Good.

Here is the second strategy. Imagine the worst.

"Wait! What? All these other gurus tell me to visualize myself doing the best that I can! Are they wrong? Why are they wrong?"

You are right, they are right, *and* I am right. First, let me explain what I mean and give you some examples. Then, at the end of the chapter, I will walk you through exactly how to do this.

When you trust me and embrace this strategy, you will grow in two ways: You will learn to control your emotions, and you will gain proper perspective.

FIRST OUTCOME:
CONTROL YOUR EMOTIONS

As you imagine the worst, you will learn to deal with those emotions in practice before you experience them in the moment. You *will* be nervous when you speak (that is a good thing which I will explain in Strategy #6.) Your anxiety will be present. The goal is to prepare yourself to be calm and collected for when the time comes.

Learn to control your emotions so that they don't control you.

To learn this ability, you must get your emotions worked up. That sounds awful, doesn't it? Yes, I experience pushback from clients when I teach this strategy. The whole reason they hire me is so they won't be anxious when they speak. Little do they realize that one key strategy to reduce anxiety when they speak is to experience that anxiety beforehand!

Think about sports, playing music, or any other type of performance. My sport growing up was soccer, so I will use this example.

Our soccer practice needed to simulate our soccer games. Our coach wanted us to play hard in the game, therefore he trained us hard. In practice, we would run longer than we did in the games. In practice, we would confront more challenges than in the games. In practice, we would take more shots than in the games.

Practices were never easy, but when game time arrived, we were ready. The coach had conditioned our bodies and minds for a grueling game. Often, this made the game far easier than the practice. Our team was so good that sometimes we shut out the other team. When that was the case, those of us who were starters ended up getting to rest and relax far more than we had at practice. We prepared as if we were playing against the hardest teams. Our preparation led to us playing much better when game time arrived.

Can you relate? Did you put hours and hours into piano practice and, as a result, the performance went smoothly? Can you remember a time when you studied for weeks and aced the exam on the big day? We know this principle: the right kind of practice prepares us for the actual event.

Think of the opposite scenario. Remember that time when you didn't prepare for the test? The day came, and when you read the questions, you barely knew what to do. Your lack of preparation led to the worst grade you ever received.

Practice gets you ready for performance.

In practice, you have time to prepare for the performance. In practice, you can tweak the skills you need to perform. In practice, you confront the physical and mental challenges you will encounter during the performance.

MENTAL AND PHYSICAL PREPARATION

Yes, you need to practice giving the speech, but you also need to practice the emotional challenge of the speech. You need to embrace this strategy. Mental, along with physical preparation will help you. Before you get up in front of people, imagine their faces. Imagine how you will feel. Imagine that you forget your notes. Imagine you say, like I did, that a woman in the audience is old. Imagine discovering your zipper is down, or your skirt is tucked into your underwear. Imagine the *worst*.

Get nervous. Get anxious. Get afraid.

Do you feel it? Good.

Now, calm yourself down. Take a deep breath. Pause. Smile. Take another deep breath. Focus on five details around you. Look at the color of the cover on this book. Notice what font I used. What is the texture of your pants? What shade of color is your shirt? Guess the temperature of the air on your skin.

Then, keep reading. Keep going. Don't stop. Don't run. Don't get up. You can do it.

During soccer practice, we prepared for the game physically. We ran. We shot at goals. We defended. But we also practiced strategies. We rehearsed pre-planned plays. We gathered around a whiteboard and discussed how we could improve teamwork. Then we physically practiced what we strategically planned. On top of this, our coach made us emotionally tough. He ran us to the point where we wanted to quit. He pushed us to block speeding balls until we wanted to duck. He yelled at us when we slowed down. He wanted us to be tough: physically, mentally, and emotionally.

You need to practice the speech and prepare yourself to handle the emotions you will encounter.

SPEAKING AT MY COUSIN'S MEMORIAL

I spoke at the memorial for my cousin who died in Iraq. Hundreds of people showed up in his home state of Oregon. The governor shared the stage with me. Military officers, dressed in their ceremonial uniforms, stood on the stage next to me. The room was full of people I didn't know, and dignitaries dotted the room. My nerves were elevated for four reasons: I was merely in my twenties, decorated leaders were following my lead, the room was full, and I had lost my younger cousin to the war.

Can you imagine the nervous energy coursing through my body? Have you ever been in such a nerve-racking setting?

As I prepared my speech, I imagined the event. I even took time to cry as I felt the emotion of losing my cousin Graham. As I rehearsed my written words out loud, I looked at the wall and imagined the stares. I breathed deeply, and finally, I smiled.

The day came. My stomach was in knots as I drove five hours to the memorial. During the drive, I rehearsed my short speech, and practiced controlling my nerves again.

As I sat near the front, preparing to speak, I stayed in the moment. I stopped my mind from asking, "What will they think of me?" Instead, I did what I had done earlier: I breathed deeply, and I smiled.

When the time came and I went up on stage, hundreds of people stared at me as I began to speak. Emotions flooded every part of my being. What did I do? Can you guess?

Once again, I breathed deeply. I smiled. And I spoke.

I was in control because I had practiced the emotions beforehand.

We perform the way we practice, so learn to practice the physical skill of speaking along with controlling the emotional currents you will experience.

SECOND OUTCOME:
IT IS RARELY AS BAD AS YOU IMAGINE

Recently, I spoke with JT, a very successful businessman. He had launched one store, and over the course of a few years, expanded his business to 48 locations. In our coaching session, he prepared a speech to give to the board of one of his competitors. After his 5-minute speech, I provided feedback, and then we launched into this same lesson I am writing to you.

"JT, will you be nervous when you speak to this group?" I asked.

"Absolutely," he said. "It's why I read the whole speech to you. Everyone sees me as confident, but when I'm in front of people, I get so nervous that I ramble."

"Why? What do you think will happen?"

As I asked that question, we dove into a hilarious dialogue about worst case scenarios: one of the guys gets up and punches him, the whole room laughs, his sweaty armpits cause the room to stink, or they all cuss him out.

JT wanted a great outcome from the speech, but at the end of the day, what is the worst he will experience? Rejection from some people he doesn't know that well. He will then go home and be with his wife, he will still have his job, he will still have his health, and he will still have his life.

Go ahead and think about the worst possible scenario. Will someone punch you as you are speaking? Someone actually did punch my dad during a speech. He survived, and he is playing with my son as I write this chapter. Will someone get up and yell at you? This happened to me; someone did yell at me during a speech. She was escorted out. I continued, a bit frazzled, but the rest of the room was very kind to me. Will someone write you an awful e-mail? Yes, I've been there. I read it and deleted it. The e-mail felt bad at the time. But years later, I don't even remember what it said. Will this ruin opportunities for future speaking engagements? Maybe it will for a short while. But if you clean the wound and learn from your mistakes, you will be even better the next time. Just don't give up.

What truly awful thing will happen to you?

Nothing. You will be okay.

Imagining the worst is about preparing for the emotions. It is also about getting proper perspective.

Undoubtedly, you have had some negative public speaking experiences. Other than the subconscious wounds that you learned to deal with in Strategy #1, you really are okay. And if you fail, or get embarrassed or rejected this next time, you will be okay.

Want to hear a funny story about my friend Todd? Todd was the student body president of his private university. On one occasion, he was invited to speak to the entire faculty. He wrote the speech, practiced it, prepared to handle his nerves, and then the day came to speak. He delivered a great speech regarding his agenda as the student body president. However, the audience had a hard time paying attention...

Todd's zipper was down the entire speech.

To make matters worse, his white dress shirt was visible through the open zipper. It appeared as if everyone was getting a private peek at his white underwear. He walked off stage after he finished his speech. One of the professors walked up to him and discreetly said, "Your zipper is down." Todd's wide eyes bolted to his pants, and the zipper was indeed wide open. White peeked through his pants as bright red lit up his face. He knew in that moment that the kind smiles of his audience were less about the agenda he pushed than the amusement he provided.

Where is Todd today? He is doing extremely well. He went on to be a public speaker, and now he works as a well-respected manager for his company, where he continues to give presentations.

Your past embarrassment doesn't define your current activities. Have a good laugh at yourself. Then, imagine the worst that could come of your public speaking. Gain the proper perspective. Honestly, everything is going to work out well.

JUST ASK THE GIRL OUT

In coaching, clients ask me all kinds of questions. Recently, Justin, a young leader with incredible potential, asked me a fun question: "Mike, I have a friend I've been hanging out with a lot. I've never thought of her romantically, but I could see a real future with her. I've been thinking of asking her out, but I don't want to ruin the friendship. What should I do?"

I responded, "Just ask her out."

You never know until you try. And if the attempt doesn't work, then let's imagine the worst-case scenario: Justin will experience rejection. The worst outcome is that she says no.

"Wait a minute, Mike. He might lose her as a friend too." That is true, but when they eventually get married to other people, he may lose her as a friend anyway. Why not risk losing her as a friend for the next couple of years for the possible outcome of gaining her as a girlfriend (and maybe future wife)?

The possible good outweighs the possible bad.

What bad outcomes could happen if you perform poorly? You might embarrass yourself and get rejected. Embarrassment will be a bummer for a while, but not forever. After all, you've been embarrassed and rejected in the past, and here you are with a passion to get better. The fact that you bought this book tells me you're doing more than okay. If you fail and fall down, then pick something up when you are down. Learn from the experience to get better for your future.

What good could come out of your event?

You could get a raise! You could honor the Bride and Groom with your toast. You could teach people about your passion. You could inspire people to make a change! You could gain respect from your peers. You could get the job, make the sale, or get promoted!

Public speaking can advance your finances, career, relationships, and life. That is a lot of good! Imagine the worst so you can prepare to combat the emotions with proper perspective. But also visualize the best! This could be the break you have been anticipating! This could be the highlight of the evening. This could be the moment where you get through to somebody!

You can do it, and you are going to be more than okay! You are not going to lose control. You are going to be in control of your emotions and use them to energize your speech, so you can influence your audience!

ACTION:
GET ANXIOUS, THEN GAIN CONTROL

How do we do this?

FIRST EXERCISE:

Imagine you are in front of your whole company, or leading a presentation, or already at your upcoming interview, or standing in front of colleagues, or teaching at your church, or giving a toast at a wedding. Picture the environment in your mind. Think about the audience members. Try to get as clear of a picture you can. If you have multiple upcoming speeches, then choose the one that makes you the most nervous.

Imagine the upcoming speech and ask yourself:

- Who will be there?

- Where will they be seated?

- Where will I stand?

- What will I be wearing?

- How many people are in the room?

- How big is the room?

- Will I have a microphone?

- Do I have a podium, lectern, music stand, table, or nothing in front of me?

- How long will my speech last?

- What mood will the people be in?

- What happens at the event before my speech?

- What will happen after I speak?

Read those questions, then close your eyes and picture yourself in the moment. Add as many details as you can. Once you can vividly imagine the event, bring in the emotions. Work yourself up. Don't avoid it. Just like we don't avoid practicing before we play the game, don't avoid practicing the emotions before the speech. Work yourself up. Get stressed.

Now, as we've discussed earlier:

1. Breathe deeply.

2. Smile.

3. Take a moment to notice five details in the room around you.

Practice this exercise regularly until you can control your emotions instead of letting them control you. (Note: if the anxiety is intense, you may have a wound that needs to be addressed with a counselor, as discussed in Strategy #1. If that is the case, schedule an appointment with a counselor immediately.)

SECOND EXERCISE:

Weigh the pros and cons of speaking. Take a blank piece of paper and draw a line down the middle with PROS at the top of one column and CONS at the top of the other.

Be very optimistic about what will happen if you do well. Visualize the best. Be detailed about the positives. Don't just write, "I could get a raise." Write down the exact amount you think you could get. Think about the positive emotions that people will experience. Be generous when you think about what good could come out of it.

Likewise, be detailed about what could go wrong. Just make sure you're as creative on the positive side of the sheet as you are with the negative.

When you finish listing the pros and cons, think about which of these will remain with you in two years. You will find that the positives have a longer shelf life than the negatives.

"Be yourself; everyone else is already taken."

Oscar Wilde

STRATEGY #3:
YOU BE YOU

Who are you? What makes you, *you?*

This is not a dissertation in philosophy so don't go too deep here. Stay shallow with me. We are not going to discover the depths of your character or the flaws of your personhood. There is a time and place for those discoveries, and they actually do matter when it comes to speaking. I often teach a lesson using a Venn diagram about how personhood combines with skills and content to create a fuller message. But, again, that is not what we are focusing on. We are focusing on public speaking strategies to overcome fear. Here is number 3: YOU BE YOU.

WHAT MAKES YOU, YOU?

What observable traits do you have? Are you tall, short, or in between? Are you dashingly handsome and trendy, or honestly normal? Are you serious? Do you talk fast? Do you like to pace? Are you energetic or a plodder? Can you readily quote interesting statistics? Are you a good storyteller? What is your DISC profile? How about your Myers Briggs? Is your voice high or low? Do you have an accent? Are you charismatic? Are you an extrovert or an introvert? Are you a family person? What is your level of education?

The questions could go on. These elements of what you do, what you enjoy, and what you look like are part of your communication. The words you say are half of your message, and *you* are the other half. If you are having a hard time tracking this train of thought, then go to YouTube and take some time to watch stand-up comedians. As you watch these professional speakers (that's ultimately what a comedian is), observe how it's not just the words they say that make them funny, it is who they are. These speakers meticulously prepare their content and then use their personhood to get their message across.

Consider some of these comedians:

- Robin Williams had the ability to imitate lots of different celebrities. He talked rapidly and used his body as part of the speech.

- Tina Fey grew up feeling out of place and awkward. Instead of pretending that she has everything together, she invites the audience into her world of understandable awkwardness.

- Chris Rock uses his very vibrant and loud voice as he retells stories and lands punch lines. He is a master of pace and cadence. He has a bright smile that disarms the audience in the midst of more graphic jokes.

- George Carlin stands in one place and communicates an intelligent, deadpan comedy. He rarely gets excited. He uses his stoic features to communicate his message.

- Drew Lynch won the heart of America on *America's Got Talent*. He had developed a stutter due to a baseball injury in high school. Instead of being embarrassed by his inability to speak fluidly, he now chooses to use it as part of his act.

- Jim Carrey used to do a lot of physical comedy.

- Demetri Martin uses random musical skills.

- Amy Poehler makes use of her signature smile.

- Ellen DeGeneres uses her own personal experiences.

- Lost Voice Guy smiles as he plays recordings of his hilarious jokes.

- Preacher Lawson shakes his butt and takes off his shirt to show his muscles.

- Mitch Hedberg showed few expressions and barely made eye contact.

Comedians are an excellent example of what it means for a speaker to make use of their own personhood in getting their point across.

WHAT DO COMEDIANS HAVE TO DO WITH OVERCOMING FEAR?

Too many speakers, presenters, toast makers, preachers, politicians, interviewees, and other communicators try to be someone they are not.

Standing in front of people and communicating a message is hard. Standing in front of people and performing as a character in a play is also difficult. In public speaking, people often combine the two. They stand up in front of people and try to communicate their message as if they are someone else. This is a recipe for fear.

Trying to be someone else in a situation like this will result in increased emotional weight: fear, anxiety, nerves, and insecurity.

THE WEIGHT OF CONTENT

You should work on creating great content and organizing it so that it flows. There are different books and different theories on how to write your speech. I often work with clients to help them organize their thoughts so that they flow well. Recently, I had the opportunity to help a client create a 20-minute presentation for a conference at M.I.T. She and I worked together for a couple of months, and she came up with a great end product that flowed from her education, experience, and expertise. Even as I gave input, direction, and edits, it was ultimately her content.

The content of your speech is a weight you carry. It could be a toast for a wedding, a presentation for your company, or a speech to announce your candidacy for office. Your message is a form of burden.

Imagine that the content/message/outline of your speech is a 10-pound dumbbell. (Don't increase the imaginary weight. You will see why in a moment.)

Have you done a front lateral raise? It's where you take the dumbbell and hold it straight out in front of you with your arm parallel to the ground. Suddenly, that 10-pound dumbbell is heavy! After a while of holding it there, your arm begins to shake. A strong, experienced weightlifter will find it easier to hold the dumbbell far away from their chest, but even then, they will get tired.

The closer you hold the dumbbell to your chest, the easier it gets. If you take the weight all the way next to you and hold it against your chest, then you can hold it for a long time.

Likewise, the more you know the content and hold it close to you, the less of a burden it becomes. (This is not about memorizing the content; it is about knowing the content. That is a big difference I teach in my courses. One is familiarity, and one is understanding.)

Know your content, and the weight of the words you say will decrease along with your nerves.

THE WEIGHT OF PERSONHOOD

My client prepared her content to speak at MIT. She organized it, she mapped it out in her mind, and she knew it. The weight of the content decreased.

Equally important as knowing the content was the need for her to be her. As we worked together using Zoom video conferencing, we would take turns presenting the material. Often I presented the material with suggestions for pauses, emphatic statements, and other speaking skills. As an experienced speaker, I tried to communicate it using her personhood. She recorded these for future review. Still, I knew that she would be tempted to imitate aspects of my personhood that came through, so I regularly cautioned her and coached her to only take elements from me that were innate to her or could easily be added on to her.

Why didn't I want her to imitate me? Because personhood is another 10-pound dumbbell.

In your left hand you have one weight, and in your right you have another. One is the content you share and the other is the personhood you communicate through. If my client tried to be me as she gave her speech, then she would be holding the right weight far from her.

Trying to speak like someone else is like holding a 10-pound weight an arm's length away from your body.

You will get tired, you will get shaky, you will feel insecure, and even if you do well, *you* didn't do well because you were being someone else.

You be you.

HOW I FAILED AND THEN FOUND 'ME'

I've been a preacher for 18 years. At one point, I even spoke over 200 times in one year. At this point in life, I now feel like I know who I am when I speak. I didn't always know. I wasn't always me.

At 26 years old, I was asked to be the main pastor for a church in Stanwood, Washington. The church was small, and they kindly asked that I transition from working with kids and youth to take on the full responsibility of the church. This meant that every week, I would be preaching for 40 minutes to a room half-filled with adults and half-filled with students. Even though this group of people had known me for years, I was nervous. I knew how to be a speaker to youth and kids. But I didn't know how to speak to the rest of the room.

That year, I embarked on a quest to discover 'me' and my voice. I read more books on speaking, and I listened to a few hundred sermons by other pastors. Each week, it seemed like I took on the personhood of the main podcast I listened to. One week, I was jovial and nonchalant like Rick Warren. The next week, I yelled a lot and told people to repent like Mark Driscoll did around 2006. Then I would become the famous preacher, TD Jakes (imagine a very white guy speaking to a small-town church in a predominantly Caucasian area, trying to be like one of the best preachers who speaks to a mainly African-American audience!). I tried to be Joel Osteen, Rob Bell, Wes Davis, Andy Stanley, Kenton Beshore, Ed Young, and several others.

That group of people was in for a ride, and they were extremely patient! (Thank you!) Our church did grow a lot that year, perhaps partly because of the show of the young preacher who had no idea what he was doing.

As I tried on each personhood, I struggled to find the real me. Then I watched this ridiculous little video called U.B.U. (https://www.youtube.com/watch?v=LQcp-J-3njw, if you are interested.) Ed Young is one of the most well-known pastors in America as he writes numerous books and leads a huge church in Dallas. He did this video for a conference his church organized. His main point was to tell speakers like me to stop trying to be someone else.

That silly video got through to me. I stopped trying to be like someone else and gave myself permission to be me. The weight of speaking suddenly decreased as I took the dumbbell of personhood and held it close to my chest.

U.B.U.

You will never be comfortable trying to be someone else.

"Mike, I don't have a story like yours. I don't have lots of people that I try to personify. All that happens when I speak is that I get really nervous!"

Yes, my story is in excess as I literally copied others and tried to take on their persona. I obviously had a problem. You too have a problem, but it's a less obvious one. Without knowing it, you have built an avatar of what you should be like when you speak. These are mental expectations, examples from people you admire in your life, industry standards, and other influences. As I work with private clients I constantly discover people shift to a new personhood when they begin to speak. Perhaps they get more serious, or louder, or change their intonation, or any other thing.

When you become an avatar of your real self, you take out the power of *you*. You also add the anxious burden of a different personhood along with the burden of your message. That is a recipe for fear.

Below, I will give you actions to take to ensure that you are being yourself. Meanwhile, take these words to heart:

Be a real version of yourself, not a poor imitation of someone else.

DO I NEED TO BE FUNNY?

That is a great question. Here is the answer: You are funnier than you realize.

I've often seen people do a negative metamorphosis when they begin their speech. I see jovial people become stoic, I watch bubbly people transform into perfect robots, I reflect how a casual person takes on a serious demeanor, and so on. The 'stage' can do something to people. It can make them act in ways unlike their usual self. In this metamorphosis, the first thing that is lost is humor.

You really are funnier than you realize. Friends will laugh with you. You joke with family members. You chuckle when you see a silly sitcom. You understand humor. But you lose it when you do your speech. How can you regain it?

Don't take yourself so seriously. I love when people prepare, plan, and perfect their speech. I love that go-getter mentality. Just make sure your perfection does not become robotic. The speech manuscript or outline is *not* the speech. *You* are the speech. The manuscript or outline is the map, but you are the guide for the listeners. I work with clients to get to know their content so they can be themselves. When you loosen the grip on your notes and learn to be at ease, then your humorous side will come out.

There are different types of humor: slapstick, one-liners, physical, observational, storytelling, etc. We often think that because we don't have all of these, it means we don't have any of these. Wrong. If you are not 'naturally' funny, learn how to insert some funny stories. If you are not 'physically' comedic, learn to give witty one-liners (even if you borrow them from others). There are 'naturally' funny people, then there are serious people who discover funny elements in life. If you go back and watch some of the stand-up comedians, you will discover both.

Do you have to be funny? No. But it does help. Humor lowers the guard of your audience. The mere act of laughter causes people to both smile and breathe deeply. Laughter relaxes your audience, which in turn relaxes you. Being funny is great, but just be *you* funny, not funny like *them*.

YOU CAN IMPROVE YOU

I want you to be you. Your speech needs you to be uniquely you. At the same time, you can improve you.

In the movie *Hitch,* Will Smith's character, Alex Hitchens, is helping his client find love with a beautiful woman. As Hitch takes his client shopping, the following dialogue takes place.

> Hitch: The shoes are hot. You went to the place I told you?
>
> Client: Yeah, but I don't think they're really me.
>
> Hitch: "You" is a very fluid concept right now. You bought the shoes. You look great in the shoes. That's the you I'm talking about.

Am I now changing my message by including this quote? Not at all. Even in the context of the movie, Hitch works for quality guys and helps them get noticed. He coaches them to improve their skills to create opportunities so that the real person stands out.

You need to be you. You can also improve and add to you. In my speech program, I teach skills such as cadence, pace, dramatic pauses, and so on. I work with clients on increasing their vocabulary, fluency, and presence. These are improvements, not replacements.

You can improve you, but you still need to be *you*.

You need to be you. Within the *you*ness, *you* is a fluid concept. You can improve you.

*You*ness and improvement is a recipe for confidence.

ACTION:
GROW INTO *YOU*

Here are three actions you can take to enact this strategy:

1. Discover You

2. Watch Yourself

3. Listen to Others

ONE: DISCOVER YOU

I highly recommend doing several personality profiles to help you understand yourself. Most personality tests won't shock you. After all, you are you. These are not meant to be a surprise; they are designed to be the honest appraisal from an intimate observer (yourself). If you do these personality profiles, read them as if you would read feedback from someone you trust.

Quick example: I always thought one of my weaknesses was impatience. Then I did the StrengthFinder and discovered that one of my strengths is being an Activator. This means that I am wired to get things done. It didn't surprise me to discover this definition of my personality, but it did reframe the way I viewed myself. While I may be impatient at times, I now try to lean into my 'get it done now' mentality. Discovering this element of myself made me appreciate my personality as a strength instead of shaming myself for my supposed weakness.

When you understand you, it helps you be you. Identify your strengths, your propensities, your natural styles of development, and your aptitudes. Discover you. Then, lean into your *you*ness.

Here are some of my favorites:

StrengthsFinder 2.0

https://www.gallupstrengthscenter.com/home/en-us/cliftonstrengths-books

Myers-Briggs. (Here is a free test.)

http://www.humanmetrics.com/cgi-win/jtypes2.asp

DISC (free test by Tony Robbins)

https://www.tonyrobbins.com/disc

TWO: WATCH YOURSELF

Give a speech to the mirror, to the computer, to your friends, or to an actual audience. Then watch yourself.

As I coach clients through Zoom video conferencing, I ask them to record their presentations. Then I give them feedback. When they watch themselves speak, they can see what I see.

Recently, I was working with a very successful business leader. His business has exploded to dozens of locations. He has a very vibrant personality and is very personable. When he started his recorded speech, his whole personhood shifted. He became serious and stale, so much so that we actually laughed about it afterwards. I said, "Who did you become?"

When you watch yourself, you can see shifts in your speaking.

Watching yourself speak is awful. When I first started, I was so embarrassed that I looked like *that* and said *that*. Few communicators enjoy listening to themselves.

Watching yourself speak is extremely useful. By watching a playback of your speech, you will be able to coach yourself!

THREE: LISTEN TO OTHERS

Why did I fall into the trap of imitation as a 26-year-old preacher? Because I excessively listened to only one speaker each week. As I begin to work with clients, one of my first recommendations is that they intentionally watch comedians, news anchors, preachers, TED talks, and some politicians.

These are five areas where a professionally trained person gets up in front of a crowd to deliver a talk. I often recommend Simon Sinek, Barack Obama, Ronald Reagan (regardless of political background), Andy Stanley, and Ellen DeGeneres. These are some great speakers who deliver with confidence. By studiously watching them and others, you can learn skills to add to your own personhood.

As I recommend speakers, undoubtedly, my clients gravitate to one or two. Caution: don't do that. Don't just listen to one speaker, no matter how incredible they are or how much you connect with them. If you listen to one, you will become a clone. And don't just listen to two. Your attention will bounce back and forth. You will see the differences and you will get confused. Listen to three or more, and *then* you will see the peculiarities of each and be able to adopt certain skills as you identify *your* style.

CLONES, CONFUSION, AND CONFIDENCE

Listen to one, and become a clone.
Listen to two, and become confused.
Listen to three or more, and gain confidence by getting better.
Learn from them. Just don't be them. Be yourself.

"Some people care too much. I think it's called love."

Winnie the Pooh

STRATEGY #4:
SPEAK TO ONE

The room had 3,200 seats. In an hour, a couple thousand people would be filling the room. I stood on stage and did a quick rehearsal of my notes. I wanted to be ready, I wanted to be prepared, and I wanted my nerves to be positive energy and not to bring on an anxiety attack. I envisioned the speech, did my mental exercises, and then I walked off the stage and prepared to meet people before the event started.

Every time I speak in front of an audience, I remind myself that I am speaking to a person, not to a crowd. Crowds are scary. People are friends. Think of it this way. Throughout history, crowds have rioted, killed, revolted, trampled, and mocked. In crowds, people lose their individual flair and take on a 'crowd mentality'. Some crowds have 10,000 people, others have 100. The size is not what makes a crowd. It is how they react. Google defines a crowd as "a large number of people gathered together in a disorganized or unruly way."

Crowds are scary.

"Mike, what are you doing? I'm already nervous, and you're making me scared!"

If you were speaking to a crowd, then you would be right. However, unless you are the president or a revolutionary, then you will never speak to a crowd. No. You are not speaking to a crowd; you are speaking to a person.

Right before I stood up to speak to the room with 3,200 seats, I went around and talked to people. I met Georgia. She is a sweet grandmother whose son played for the Seattle Seahawks. Coming from Seattle, I knew who he was, and she was delighted to hear that.

I also met Chad. Chad and I spoke for a bit. He was recently single and was trying to figure out the best steps ahead.

Tim and Sandy were a smiling couple who held hands while holding hot cups of coffee. They were recently married and had a spark of energy coming off of them.

Emily was a teenager who came to hear me speak on the topic of relationships. She was bubbly and a little bit nervous to talk to the speaker.

Isaac was fresh out of jail and needed to reboot his view on relationships. He was a bit skeptical, and yet was hoping to hear something that would inspire him and give him practical steps to take.

All the way up to when the event started, I stood out front and talked to people. I shook their hands. We introduced ourselves. When they discovered that I was the speaker, some were surprised and even nervous that the main speaker was talking to them so casually. I learned a bit of their stories. They asked for a bit of mine.

The crowd dematerialized, because I met the individuals that would soon sit next to each other to form a large audience. When I finally stood on stage, I was not speaking to a crowd, nor was I speaking to a large audience. I stood on stage and spoke to Georgia, Chad, Tim, Sandy, Emily, and Isaac. I spoke to my new friends. I wanted to speak to *them*. I communicated my points to the audience as if I was speaking to those few that I knew.

Now I wasn't speaking into the void, I was speaking into their lives.

SPEAK TO ALL
AS IF YOU ARE SPEAKING TO ONE

This is always my strategy. If I have any opportunity to personally and intimately connect with my audience first, then I take it. I don't want to speak to a room. I want to add value, educate, inform, entertain, and instruct people.

An organization reached out to me to speak to 80 sixth graders and their parents about science. Honestly, *that* was more nerve-racking than speaking to a few thousands adults! Sixth graders can be sassy, sarcastic, and ruthless. If you show weakness, they will pounce on you and tear you apart.

There was another reason I was nervous: Science. Science? I was asked to speak in regards to "science". What did that mean?

I created more rough drafts for this vague topic than perhaps any other speech I've delivered.

Is that your story? Are you speaking to an audience you don't understand? Are you speaking about a topic that is not your strength? Are you doing both?

Then, hold on, this will help you.

The week of the event came, and I drove 2 hours to the campground where the school administration had organized a 3-day field trip for 80 of the sixth graders, along with faculty and parents. I played an inspirational book in my car as I drove. Fears swirled through my mind: What if the kids hate me? What if the parents think I'm not worth it? What if the teachers see through my lack of knowledge? I was supposed to be inspiring kids toward science, and my own preparation had led me to be inspired. (Side note: You are always the first audience of your own speech.) Yet, I worried that all my preparation and experience was going to fail me.

I arrived early and settled in. My nerves had also settled in. I was afraid. I was scared. I was worried. I was in uncharted territory.

As the school buses arrived, I stood ready to act on my own strategy. As kids, teachers, and parents dismounted from the bus, I pushed past the awkwardness and introduced myself to as many people as I could: Noe, Kiesha, Alexander, Kye, Drew, Mr. Peterson, Samuel, Samuel's dad, and other. The buses unloaded, and the camp provided dinner. The first session would be right after. Because I had prepared extensively for my speech, I didn't need to escape to rehearse my outline. Doing so would have simply isolated myself with my nerves. Instead, I kept meeting people. I sat with a table of sixth graders, who were standoffish at first. However, I stayed and kept trying. Kye finally opened up about his hobbies, and then his friends joined. Finally, I connected with someone. Now I wouldn't have to speak to a crowd, I could speak to Kye.

That night, I spoke outdoors to an amphitheater filled with kids and adults. I could barely see their faces in the darkness of the night, but I could recall their faces in my mind. I didn't try to speak to a crowd, I spoke to the small group with whom I had connected. That connection made all the difference. Because I connected with few, I was able to connect with the whole class. The sixth graders listened! They leaned in. They wanted more. I had achieved my goal.

After the camp ended, the director asked parents and teachers to rate the speaker (me) in several categories. With a few mediocre exceptions, parents and teachers overwhelmingly gave me incredible ratings, and some even rated my talks as their favorite part. I had succeeded with connecting with my audience.

"Good job, Mike. But you obviously have been doing this for a while. And it sounds like you're an extrovert. This doesn't help me."

This strategy can help you and it will.

WHO IS YOUR AUDIENCE?

One of my public speaking clients was preparing to speak to forty business leaders before dinner. The room would be full of mostly men. They were characterized as wealthy, skeptical, disconnected, and 'douchey'. My client described them as the type of people she would never be friends with. Yet here she was, getting ready to speak to them. As she detailed who they were, it became clear that they were a *crowd*. I stopped her and asked if she personally knew any of them or anyone like them. She did. She knew one of the guys. I asked her to think about his story, his desires, his fears, his needs, his family, and his reason for being there.

The crowd dematerialized as she thought about this man she was acquainted with. She imagined the stress he was under with his job. She thought about the burden he felt due to his work environment. She began to understand his hopes and desires for her presentation.

We finished this exercise. Then I said, "As a whole, you may be right. This crowd might be disconnected and 'douchey'. But each of them has stories like the one you know. Don't speak to a crowd, but imagine that each one is like him. Then you are speaking to a room full of people that you sympathize with, instead of a room of men you want nothing to do with."

PERCEPTION AFFECTS RECEPTION

I had a classmate in college who didn't like me. She didn't say it, but I knew it. Can you relate? Have you been around someone who says the right words, but you still know that they don't like you? Have you worked with someone who seemed to avoid you, and you didn't know why? We can perceive how others feel towards us.

One day, I got to class early and simply said, "You don't like me. Why?"

The direct confrontation shocked her and she stammered, "What-what do you mean?"

"Every time we talk, your expressions seem distant. It feels like you just want to get away, and that somehow I offend you. Did I do something to you?"

We had a brief conversation, and it turns out I was right. She didn't like me. She was holding something against me that I hadn't even done. She purposefully distanced herself because of her distaste. I perceived it, and it affected how I received her words. Once I was able to correct her poor perception of me, it changed her reception. We became friends, and then we dated. (Eventually, we broke up. That is an entirely different story, though.)

Your feelings toward your audience affect how they will feel towards you.

Your perception of who the audience is will affect their reception of your speech.

How do you ensure your feelings are positive? By getting to know some of them. If that is impossible, try to imagine who they are; create three characters with backstories and speak to those personal connections in the audience. If you like them, they will be more likely to like you. If they like you, then you will feel that as well, and it will ease your nerves.

It is extremely important that you like your audience. "Mike, I don't know them." You have to create a sense that you do. At the minimum, find one person in the room, or make one up, and speak to one.

Speak to one and work to like at least one more.

"Mike, when I speak to you, your eyes gloss over, and so I stop talking." He was right. We had a history, and due to how I perceived him, I didn't receive him. It didn't matter what he said; if it went longer than a short chat, I started tuning him out.

Do you want your audience to tune you out?

"I don't really care. I just want to get through my speech."

Your speech will be miserable if your audience tunes you out. Just like he hurried to finish talking with me when I tuned him out, so will *you* feel rushed if your audience tunes you out. Don't just get through your speech to a crowd. Don't do that. Instead, connect with someone and talk to that person. Give your toast to a guest you met at the wedding. Give your presentation at work as if you are talking to your lunch buddy. When you stand in front of a room to honor an employee, imagine your spouse is in the room and that you are speaking to them about your employee.

> # #ProTip:
>
> ## Talk to the one, but look at many.

MAKE IT PERSONAL

Did you watch *You've Got Mail*, starring Tom Hanks and Meg Ryan? If so, you know about an online chat they have. Meg's character is struggling with an issue, and Tom responds with a phrase born from the movie *The Godfather*, "You've got to take it to the mattresses." Which means it isn't personal.

Don't we feel that way about a lot of speeches?

- It's not personal, it's professional.

- This is not about people, it's about the product.

- Revenue is at stake, relationships are secondary.

- I'm not doing this for friends, I'm doing this for the teacher who is making me do it.

In *You've Got Mail*, Tom's advice ended up being wrong. His own advice hurt him, and at some point, Meg wisely teaches us that there is rarely such a thing as "not personal". She looks at her business competitor and says, "Well, it was personal for me."

Don't take your speech to the mattresses. Don't make it just about business. Even if your setting is the most academic or professional, you are not speaking to dollar bills or tomes of literature. You are speaking to people.

You can choose to communicate as if to buildings and books, because they won't make you feel nervous. But they won't listen to you, either.

You can communicate with anything, but that doesn't mean you can connect with anything. You don't connect with a crowd; you connect with a person. So, go out of your way to make the big room small by speaking to all as if you were speaking to one.

ACTION:
DO THIS CHECKLIST

What should you do before your presentation, sales pitch, or other speech?

I'll explain my 6-Point checklist, then I'll put a longer list on a separate page so you can copy it or take a picture for you to look at before the event.

1. Do IT EARLY: ARRIVE EARLY AND PREPARE EARLY.

When you create space, you create peace.

Learn the art of doing everything early.

Finish all additional preparation early. Think through what props you will need. Get them now. Think through any tech you will need. Order it. Get to the space early. Walk the stage. Check out the room. Test the mic. Do a rehearsal.

No matter how small or how big, you want to finish all the preparation early: slides, props, pictures, room setup, tables, booklets, merchandise, food, and print two copies of your notes.

Extremely important: Get your speech done ahead of time. Don't cram.

#ProTip

Always print two copies of your notes. Even if one is electronic, print another. Trust me, it will make you sleep better.

Arrive early. Having margin in your schedule allows you to not feel rushed. Some speakers fail at this. They don't want to think about the upcoming speech, so they book their day and run from place to place right up to their speech. Avoid this recipe for ruin. Rushing around increases our stress and nerves. Sure, you might get to your speech sooner, but it won't make you feel better. It won't make your connection deeper. It won't leave you feeling good afterward.

"Hurry up, then wait."

I have said those words so many times. I use it for myself to get all my work done in advance. I use it for organizing trips to

Senegal and Mexico (through the organization I chair, https://www.goonthemission.com). I use it as I coach people. Now, I share it with you:

Hurry up now, so that you can have space and wait later.

2. DON'T DRINK COFFEE WHILE YOU ARE WAITING, ESPECIALLY IF YOU ARE NERVOUS. DRINK TEA.

Full disclosure: I do drink coffee. I live in the Seattle area. I've also been doing this for a long time.

Here's what I do avoid. I stay away from sugar before I speak. Sugar and coffee both temporarily increase your energy. When you are anxious, you already have nervous energy flowing through your body. Combine the negative energy of fear with the amped-up energy of caffeine and sugar... and your senses overload with bad vibrations.

It's hard enough to handle nerves, so don't stir in sugar and caffeine to create a pre-stage concoction.

3. STAND WHERE YOU CAN MEET A FEW PEOPLE.

Often, a speaker will stand apart from the audience. Don't do that. Get in there with the people. I have a simple rule about this: STAND 5 FEET AWAY FROM THE WALL.

Next time you are at a public gathering, watch where people stand. They move to the wall. It's safe there. It's out of the way. It's protective. Most people and many speakers like to be next to the protective cover of the wall, and they also like to take cover behind cell phones or cups of coffee.

My "5-Feet Rule" reminds me to get away from the protective covering of the wall. It reminds me to get *in* the way of people instead of getting away from them. Embrace this rule, and people will feel like you are embracing them.

4. SMILE.

Smiling enhances your attractiveness, which enhances your confidence.

Smiling is a natural antidepressant. The act of smiling enhances the way your neural communication functions, and it releases neuropeptides along with dopamine and serotonin.

Smiling reduces your blood pressure. Try it! Go to the store and sit at one of those little tables that take your blood pressure. Then smile for a full minute and try again.

Smiling actually boosts your immune system!

When you smile, your brain chemistry alters, your nerves decrease, your voice strengthens, and your audience feels it. Smiling connects you to other people. Smiling relaxes the recipients of your speech, and will even cause them to smile back.

I can't stress this enough. It is the number one advice I give. Smile.

5. BREATHE DEEPLY.

"Deep breathing increases the supply of oxygen to your brain and stimulates the parasympathetic nervous system, which promotes a state of calmness." (https://www.stress.org/take-a-deep-breath)

There is ample research if you want to dive into how deep breathing can improve multiple areas of life. Do a quick web search and you will be convinced.

When it comes to speaking, you don't need to understand all the science; just know that it will calm you. Calm people connect on a deeper level than stressed people. For you to connect with your group, learn the practice of deep breathing.

- Inhale through the nose. Exhale through your mouth.

- Pray or meditate.

- Download an app called *Breathe* and follow its instructions.

6. MAKE IT YOUR MISSION TO CONNECT WITH 3-5 PEOPLE.

You can meet more, but create a connection with 3-5 people. I showed how I do this at the beginning of this strategy. It's not enough to know the names of a few. You need to *know* a few.

Politicians and preachers are a great illustration of this principle. The congregation of a church may vary week to week.

However, some of the people in the church are there almost every week, and most share a belief structure. Politicians speak to different crowds as they campaign. However, some firm believers go on the road each week, and most are marked by shared philosophy of governance. As a result, the preacher or politician feels more at ease because they know and understand the person they speak to. They are connected on a relational front and a profound ideologue.

If you have to speak to your school, coworkers, shark tank, wedding party, shareholders, or investors, work hard to find ways to connect with them before you speak a word up front.

Stay in the moment with people, and don't get ahead of yourself. Be right with the person you are talking to. Smile at them. Practice active listening where you hear what they say and use what they say when you reply to them.

Avoid looking beyond the person you are with. Make *that* person the most important one. If you need to excuse yourself so you can connect with others, then simply express your need: "It's been great talking to you, Sam. Thank you for sharing the story of what brought you here. Please excuse me as I connect with a few more people before we begin. And thank you for being here!"

Forget for a moment that you are going to communicate *to* people and work to connect *with* people.

When you start speaking, speak to people, not to the crowd.

When it's time for you to get up in front of 10 people or 100 people or 1000 people. Forget about the number. Find your new friends and do your presentation to them. And don't forget to smile.

MY CHECKLIST

☐ I will ensure that I finish all preparation at least an hour

☐ before my speech.

☐ I will arrive early.

☐ I will not get hyped on coffee or sugar.

☐ I will stand away from the wall to meet people.

☐ I will smile.

☐ I will breathe deeply.

☐ I will connect with 3-5 people.

☐ I will not be worried; I will stay in the moment with people.

☐ I will speak to PEOPLE, not to the crowd.

☐ I will make sure that I smile.

☐ I will be okay.

"Never be so busy as not to think of others."

Mother Teresa

STRATEGY #5:
IT'S NOT ABOUT YOU

The moment you have been dreading is here. You are about to stand in front of people. You are about to try to get your points across. You are about to have all eyes on you. Your mind begins to race…

"What will they think of me? Will they listen to me? Will they like me? Do they trust me? Do I know what I'm saying? Do I look okay? Is my fly down? No, my fly is not down. Glad I checked for the 7th time. Do I have lipstick on my teeth? I bet I have lipstick on my teeth. Oh wait, I don't wear lipstick. Do I have lettuce in my teeth? Everyone is going to be looking at me! Oh shoot, what if I smell bad? What if I forget my notes? What if someone gets up and walks out on me? I'm going to be terrible. They're going to see right through me! I hate speaking in front of people!"

Have you experienced an inner monologue like this? Have you wondered what your audience thought of you or what they will think about you? Of course you have. When all eyes are on us, we feel scrutinized. We feel judged. We feel like we are under a microscope.

Here's the good news. People think about you far less than you could imagine.

PEOPLE ARE NOT THINKING OF YOU

You are worried about what people are thinking about you, but meanwhile, they aren't thinking about you... they are worried what you are thinking about them!

The movie *What Women Want* debuted in 2000, starring Mel Gibson and Helen Hunt. The movie depicts Mel's character as a stereotypical male chauvinist who suddenly gains the power to hear what women are thinking. In one scene Mel gets up to pitch his idea to a boardroom. As he works to get his message across, he is struck by the discovery that even though everyone is looking at him, they are thinking about different concerns. Their eyes are on him; their thoughts are not.

What Mel experienced in the movie is the reality we face each time we talk to a group. People are far less concerned about you than you fear. I can personally attest to this. I'm guilty of doing this on numerous occasions. I have been in the audience for many different types of presenters: comedians, salespersons, preachers, teachers, leadership presenters, coaches, valedictorians, and a myriad of other people who have stood up to talk. While I try to think about the content of their words, I've often been swept away by a wide variety of thoughts: "Will this be helpful to me? I like math more than biology. I should plan my upcoming vacation. He looks so confident... I wonder what I look like. Shoot—my fly is down!" And so on. See, while the presenter is often afraid of what people think about her, the audience is more concerned thinking about themselves.

WE ARE OUR FAVORITE FOCUS

Try not to argue this point. We could read any number of psychologists that address our obsession with self. Let's leave that to another book. Instead, just answer this: what is your first thought when you wake up? It's probably one of three: "I don't want to get up, I just want one more minute of sleep…" or for the morning go-getters, "It's morning! Yay. I'm excited for the day!" and for everyone else, "I have to pee!!!"

What do those three morning thoughts have in common? Waking up is all about *you*. Your first thought is not taking care of poor people in West Africa. Your first thought is not hoping your colleague does a great job at work. Your first thought is you. And that's okay. My first thought is about me. We are the only ones fully responsible for our lives, so we ought to have a healthy focus on ourselves.

Agree that you think of you, a lot. Then begin to realize that your audience is not thinking of you. This will free you up. When you realize that the people in front of you care less about your content than they do about their own hair, clothes, hunger, and sleep, then it allows the pressure of the moment to fade. Take a deep breathe. Serve your audience by entertaining, educating, or presenting your product. They will be far less concerned with how you do and much more preoccupied with their own thoughts.

HOW MANY TIMES DID THE 2ND PARAGRAPH SAY "I/ME"

"What will they think of **me**? Will they listen to **me**? Will they like **me**? Do they trust **me**? Do **I** know what **I'm** saying? Do **I** look okay? Is **my** fly down? No, **my** fly is not down. Glad **I** checked for the 7th time. Do **I** have lipstick on **my** teeth? **I** bet **I** have lipstick on **my** teeth. Oh wait, **I** don't wear lipstick. Do **I** have lettuce in **my** teeth? Everyone is going to be looking at **me**! Oh shoot, what if **I** smell bad? What if **I** forget **my** notes! What if someone gets up and walks out on **me**? **I'm** going to be terrible. They're going to see right through **me**! **I** hate speaking in front of people!"

How many times? 25.

When you scrutinize yourself, you will find every flaw.

When you scrutinize yourself, you imagine others are paying the same amount of attention that you do. They aren't. They are worried about themselves. They are hoping that *their* needs will be met.

People are hoping to get something from your speech that will fit into their life: they want to be entertained by your hosting, they want to be moved by your toast, they want to gain insight from the presentation, they want to be inspired by your speech, they don't want to have to work more due to your proposal, they want to make their own life better by buying into your sales pitch, they want to understand the direction of their workplace by your vision casting, or they want to gain market share by sitting in your session.

They want something that is best for *them*.

How many times did "I" or "me" fit in the last two paragraphs? Zero.

It's about them. It's not about you.

PEOPLE WANT YOU TO SUCCEED

"No, they don't. They are jealous, competitive, and undermining." Okay. A few people don't want you to succeed. If your promotion hinges on your presentation in direct competition with the presentation of a co-worker, then the other person doesn't want you to succeed. But they aren't your audience.

The vast majority of your audience wants you to do well. If you have an enemy in the crowd, block them out. There are too many people cheering you on to focus on the one lowlife person who is focused on jeering at your work. Life is too short to try to please the haters. In the words of the philosopher Taylor Swift, "Shake It Off."

What will people think about when they see you in front? They will primarily think of how this will affect their own life. Secondarily, they will want you to do well. They will be subconsciously, if not consciously, rooting for you. That is why we applaud when someone finishes well. We are pleased that their performance didn't make us feel awkward. It is also why we shift in our seats if a speaker loses their place in their talk.

Have you been there? Have you been in that awkward moment?

As you listen to a speaker present, suddenly you realize that he loses his place in his speech. The room silences. People shift in their seats. Faces turn red. The speaker starts repeating words and begins to use lots of "umms" and "errs". Maybe some kind person goes over to help the speaker out. You whisper to the person next to you, "I feel bad for him."

We feel bad for the person who doesn't succeed at speaking. It causes us to feel embarrassed, uncomfortable, and awkward.

See what happened there? Even the success or failure of a speaker is about us. People are thinking of you *far* less than you imagine. When they do, they want you to succeed, because your success is their success.

My friend Micah called me one afternoon. We caught up on family life and then he gave me the update, "Here's the big thing going on in my life. Our company's owner has sold the tech firm. I'm about to have a new boss."

"What do you think? Is this a good thing?" I asked.

"I hope so. Not sure yet. There are some changes that need to take place, and I hope he can make that happen."

Have you been there? Have you had a top leader replaced by a new leader? Whether you liked the previous leader, you at least knew what she was like. Now, a new leader becomes the CEO, your supervisor, the pastor of your church, the principal of your school, or the president of your country. As you think about these transitions, let me ask you the same question I asked Micah, "What do you think? Is this a good thing?" I bet your response would be similar to Micah's: "I hope so!" Why do we hope we will like new leaders? Because hoping the leader fails is like hoping your pilot crashes simply because you dislike him. Regardless of how we feel about our leaders and our speakers, we need them to do well because it affects... *us!*

People want you to succeed. Your success is their success. If you make it about them, then they will like you all the more.

FOCUS DETERMINES DIRECTION

15-year-old Mike Acker gripped the wheel of the beaten-up Pontiac.

I was learning to drive. My car cruised over to the centerline and repeatedly ran over the yellow turtles embedded in the asphalt. The instructor gently pulled the wheel to the right and offered the sage advice, "Where you look is where you will go." I had focused on the centerline so I kept driving on the centerline. With his words in mind, I lifted my gaze. I concentrated on a point far ahead of me. The car straightened out.

I'm sure that the instructor has no idea how his driving advice impacted my life. I have thought of those words in many areas of life. I have used them for coaching goal setters, business owners, executives, and speakers.

What you focus on is where you are headed.

If you stand on stage and focus on how well *you* are doing, then you will be nervous, concerned, and fearful. You will feel like everyone is thinking of you, judging you, and critiquing you. Remember, just because all eyes are on you does not mean that all the attention is on you. They see you and they hear you, but they are thinking of themselves.

Shift your focus. Think about them. How can you help them? How can you instruct them? How can you lift them up? How can you educate them? How does your pitch serve them?

WHAT IS YOUR GOAL?

Rarely is the goal of public speaking, "I want everyone to see how amazing I am." If that is the goal, then most likely it will be a short-lived career. Think of some of these engagements where people get in front of others to speak. What is their goal?

Take notice how the goal starts with "I" or "MY", then moves to helping people.

MC

- I want everything to flow well for the event and to put the organizers at ease.

- My speaking helps people.

SALES

- I believe in my product or service. If my audience buys it, then it will help them.

- My sales pitch helps people.

AUCTIONEER

- People are coming because they want to buy something. It's not about me.

- My presenting helps people get what they want.

PREACHER

- I believe in my message. My congregation needs to understand these points.

- My preaching gives guidance, hope, and life.

POLITICIAN

- I understand what needs to be done. My people need representation.

- My campaigning will bring hope and positive change. I help people.

PRESENTER

- I understand a key component of our business. My coworkers need this.

- My presentation updates the team and satisfies my boss. I am part of a team.

TOAST

- The bride and groom are friends. They mean a lot to me. I was asked to speak.

- My words bring up fun memories and encouraging thoughts. I honor them.

EXECUTIVE

- My company and employees need vision. I need to address our people.

- My vision casting will bring alignment, clarity, and unity. I help people.

Yes, these goals start with I/my. After all, we are responsible for our part. Then, the goal maker connects the dots from I/my to *them*. That is what will make these speeches more effective and less nerve-racking.

We could do this with any type of speech: school, business, entertainment, civic, military, or any other area. The goal of any type of speech can be to help people and to serve the audience you address.

Are there some people out there with a goal to serve themselves? Sure. Usually, we can see through them and we are not drawn to them. In those rare cases, eventually the weight of fame and self-imposed glory crashes in on them. Their goal was to be liked and one unfriendly comment drives them into despair. This is not you. Don't let your big goal be a desire to be liked. Discover how your speech, presentation, or talk helps others.

Ask yourself: how can I help, serve, entertain, inform, educate, or inspire *them*? I want to serve *them*. The irony is that when you focus on them, they begin to like you.

GET IN THEIR HEAD

Before you speak, connect the dots. Take a moment, a day, or a week and consider these questions:

- Why are you speaking? (Desire, obligation, duty)

- What do they need or want?

- How can you give that to them?

- Who is your audience?

Then get in the head of the audience members:

- What are their hopes and dreams?

- What are their fears?

- What do you have that you can give them? (Motivation, tips, information, laughter…)

- Why are they listening to you?

- What are they even more concerned about?

- What hidden worries do you think they might have? (Develop empathy for them)

- How can you add value?

Leadership guru, John Maxwell, tells a great story about the time he was a keynote speaker at a charity golf event. The organizers of the event had planned too much content and not enough breaks for the attendees. The speakers leading up to John Maxwell seemed more intent on finishing their own prepared content than the fact that the audience was exhausted. After the second to last speaker finished, the host introduced John Maxwell. Normally a huge round of applause would receive him. But people were tired. And people care more about themselves than the person on stage. John walked to the stage and read the audience. What do you think he saw?

He looked at the attendees. They didn't *need* any more. They didn't *want* any more. He was caught in a dilemma. He was being paid to speak and he was the speaker with the biggest name at the event. What would he do? Would he make this about his speech or the people?

As he walked to the stage he surveyed the crowd and then spoke: "It's been a long day and a long program. Most of us are tired. My leadership talk is the following: everything rises and falls on leadership." That was it. He was done.

After this extremely short talk, he walked off the stage and sat down. There was silence for a moment as the audience processed what happened. Then suddenly, the people began a thunderous round of applause with a standing ovation. It wasn't what he said as he spoke, it was *who* he valued when he spoke.

Embrace this strategy and here is what you will find:

The more you value your audience, the more they will value you.

The more you serve your audience, the less worried you will be about your performance.

The more you focus *on* them, the less fearful you will be of them.

ACTION:
GO THE EXTRA MILE

As you turn the focus of the speech from you to them, here are some ways you can go the extra mile before and after you present.

1. Plan to do more.

2. Learn to listen.

3. Discover their thoughts.

ONE: PLAN TO DO MORE.

Consider what additional elements you can do before, during, or after the event. Be inspired by how Ellen DeGeneres and Oprah Winfrey give away gifts, and it makes people love them!

- Can you send handwritten cards?

- What about calling some of the audience members before or after?

- What giveaways can you provide?

- What about snacks, candy, or beverages?

- Is there an item that fits your speech and can be handed out to even one person?

- Can you provide notebooks, pens, or books for your event?

- How about offering one free service to the group?

- Would a picture enhance your speech? A video? A token for everyone?

TWO: LEARN TO LISTEN.

When I coach business clients, we often focus on this key principle: leaders are listeners. Speaking in public is a form of leadership. Afterall, leadership boils down to influence. When you give a presentation, a talk, a message, or a speech, then you are trying to influence emotions, actions, and understanding. If leaders need to listen and speakers are leaders, then speakers need to listen! Learn to listen.

Listening not only helps you make the speech about *them* instead of about you (which, as you know, will help reduce your fear,) it also improves your ability to read the audience, know what to avoid, understand where to dwell, and realize when it is time to end early! Listening helps you perform, gesture, smile, breathe, grow, mature, and learn. Learn to listen.

#ProTip:

Regardless of how well you are with public speaking, if you want to get better in life, then learn to listen.

The most brilliant leaders, scientists, politicians, philosophers, counselors, pastors, teachers, comedians, and other speakers work hard to master the art of observation. This ability to listen to nature, to social concerns, to influencers, and to other phenomena gives them something to speak about. When they speak, they are more interesting because they are able to offer insight about the world around us. Listening to others makes you more interesting.

Listening makes you more intelligent. As Larry King, the award-winning television host, stated, "I remind myself every morning: Nothing I say this day will teach me anything. So if I'm going to learn, I must do it by listening." Listening will grow you.

Listening will also make you *seem* more intelligent. There is an ancient wisdom adage found in the book of Proverbs, chapter 17, verse 28: "Even a fool who keeps silent is considered wise; when he closes his lips, he is deemed intelligent." (ESV translation)

Listening creates empathy for those you work with. When you understand people, you know how to speak to them. If you take time to listen, you will understand the concerns, fears, and worries they feel. Listening shifts the focus from YOU to them. If you want to ease your fear of public speaking, learn to listen. After all, it's not about you.

This week, practice your listening skills. I must admit, I write this to myself as well. I have not mastered this area. I am growing with you. Let's commit this week to increasing our listening muscles. Take some time to act on this exercise:

- Who are five people you can learn more about this week (maybe from your future audience)? Get to know their back-story, their goals, and their dreams.

THREE: DISCOVER THEIR THOUGHTS.

This strategy teaches you the importance of understanding others. Take a moment to act on this strategy as you reflect on an upcoming opportunity to speak to others. Take out a notebook or open a new document. Then write out some answers for the following questions. As you think more about them, take note of how your goal shifts from your performance to helping people. (For an extended lesson on three of these questions, go to https://3and3.stepstoadvance.com/book.)

- Why are you speaking?

- What does your audience need or want?

- How can you give it to them?

- Who is your audience?

- What are their hopes and dreams?

- What are their fears?

- What do you have that you can give them?

- Why are they listening to you?

- What are they even more concerned about?

- What hidden worries do you think they might have?

- How can you add value?

"Where focus goes, energy flows."

Tony Robbins

CHANNEL THE POWER

"Mike, how long did it take before you stopped being nervous when you went onstage?" This is a common question I receive.

Here is my answer that I am proud to give: I'm nervous every time.

"You mean that if I employ these seven strategies I will still be nervous? Then what's the point?"

Here is what I promise. When you employ these seven strategies, your fear will *not* be completely erased; it will be thoroughly eased. That is a good thing. Don't get rid of your nervousness, but learn to channel it.

LOU TAUGHT ME HOW TO PUNCH

In 2011, Taylor and I moved to a new city as I took on a new job. I was hired as the president to turn around a non-profit organization with millions of dollars of debt and a dwindling customer base. It was a mammoth responsibility. Because the job initially brought me a pay cut, my wife took on a second job. This allowed me to work seven days each week to overcome the missteps of the past, work on the financial situation, reorganize our departments, repair relationships with past clientele, and remodel our building. There was a lot going on at the same time. There was a lot of stress inherent in the role.

How do you handle stress?

Stress is a form of negative energy that can bring about all sorts of health problems, eating disorders, and sleepless nights. I could *feel* the stress in my body. One day I met with Lou who had been a part of the staff. He then ran a mixed martial arts academy. He invited me to train for free. Three times per week, I would meet with him in the morning for personal training. He taught me how to kick and how to punch. He worked me hard. At times, I threw up when I overdid it. He would have me work the heavy bags for two-minute intervals, then run stairs, then do pushups, etc. Each day he pushed me. As my energy flowed into my jabs, push kicks, and sparring sessions, I noticed that the negative stress energy dissipated. I discovered that I could channel the negative energy of stress into the positive energy of a workout.

TRANSFORM BAD INTO GOOD

When I channeled negative energy into a positive outcome, I began to sleep better, eat better, look better, and feel better. Anything can be better when you use something potentially negative for a positive outcome:

- My dad worked hard to turn a negative childhood into a positive one for my sister and me. His negative experience and fear of failure became the impetus for him to learn how to do it the right way.

- Wise generals do this in the military. They study negative outcomes and strategize how to use past mistakes to educate them on how to have victories for the future.

- Smart students use this tactic with school. They learn what they did wrong and channel that fear of repeating a bad grade into energy to ensure they will get a good grade in the future.

- Competitive athletes work hard to turn losses and poor performance into wins and strengths.

- Even the strength of rivers can be channeled into a hydroelectric dam to create energy for power grids and contain the flow of the river.

Leadership guru and mentor, John Maxwell, puts it this way: "When you are down, pick something up."

We see this phenomenon all throughout our lives. Negative energy can be channeled for a positive purpose.

ENERGY IS THE FLIPSIDE OF FEAR

Your fear can be channeled into energy for your speech, interview, or any other form of speaking. Don't erase your fear; ease your fear. Then use the rest of that raw energy to electrify your communication.

If you erase your fear, then you will eliminate the energy that makes you interesting.

Have you seen a boring speaker? They probably know their content very well. They are probably an expert. They regularly get up to speak in front of the organization they started, or in the room they teach in each year, or in front of their church, or in front of their co-workers. These boring communicators take the audience for granted. They assume the audience is interested just because people are present. They don't work to connect; they just work to give you their content.

Why is it that some speakers are boring? Here is one of the reasons: they stopped caring about the outcome.

One reason why you are worried, scared, nervous, and terrified to speak is because you care. You care about doing well. You care about getting your message across. You care about what people think.

Why do some speakers put you to sleep? They became complacent.

If you do want to completely dissolve your nerves, anxiety, and fear, I will teach you how right here. I don't recommend this, but it will work. Become complacent. A quick Google definition of complacency gives us this picture: "Showing smug or uncritical satisfaction with oneself or one's achievements." If you want to erase fear, get prideful. If you want to get rid of anxiety in speaking, decide that you are amazing and that it is an honor for people to listen to you. If you take on an air of arrogance, you will erase your nerves... and become irrelevant.

Instead of completely erasing your fear of speaking, turn your nervous care into focused energy.

WHO DO YOU CARE ABOUT?

My wife will be my worst enemy if she has to testify in court about my driving.

Growing up in Mexico, I learned to drive in Mazatlan, a large city that had few stoplights at the time. To drive was to drive aggressively. There was no alternative. If you waited for others, you would be waiting in your driveway until you were dead. You had to learn to objectify people as mere cars that you were combatting with to gain superiority.

I learned to drive in Mexico and then moved to the United States. More than 20 years later, I still objectify people the moment they get into their car. Just recently, Taylor and I left our home in separate cars. She left first with our son. I caught up to her. She was a moment late in accelerating through a green light. I got frustrated with the "stupid car" in front of me. Then I realized it was my wife and son! I am an aggressive driver who cares more about himself than the other "stupid cars" around me. I'm working on it.

On my way home one day when I was 22, I was cruising along at 35 miles an hour (maybe 50… shhh.) Approaching an intersection with a green light for my lane, I kept going forward. The center turn lane was stacked with cars. A Ford Explorer coming the opposite way patiently waited for an opening to turn left across my lane. Some kind, oblivious person waved the

Explorer through. The stupid Explorer didn't think to check my lane and crossed my lane at the exact time I was driving through.

CRASH. BANG. BOOM. (All the comic book noises here.) #$@%. &^!!!$. !@*%. (Some of the expletives here.) My shiny new hatchback collided into the stupid Explorer. My aggressive side came out: "What an idiot!!! Who doesn't watch where they are going?" I thrust the car door open and leapt outside. My nerve endings were filled with raw power. I was ready to get in the driver's face to give them the full force of my irritation.

A young mom stepped out of the driver's side. She was crying. She ran to the door that caught the weight of my car. She threw out an "I'm sorry" to me as she ran past. Thankfully, I had the grace to shut up. She drew upon Wonder Woman's strength and yanked the crumpled door open to check on the toddler sitting behind the battered side of the car.

Oh wait, I didn't crash into a car. I collided with people. In that moment, my negative energy became compassionate care. I *ran* to her and ignored her apologies. What could I do to help? The little girl was crying. Another child was talking incessantly. The mom was frantic. I threw all my energy into making sure they were okay. I helped her move the car and her family out of the road.

The little girl was okay. And so was I. The mom and I traded information, reported the incident to the police, and moved on with life. As I drove my limping car away (which had to be totaled), I gained a realization. My fury and rage can be used to help people, not hurt them with words and aggression. We can use passion to help people.

"Good for you, Mike."

Thank you.

"What does that have to do with me?"

Everything. Channel the powerful energy of worry to productive energy of prayer or positive thinking. Channel the exhausting energy of anxiety into the promising energy of listening. Channel the negative energy of fear into the exciting energy of presenting your material.

Learn to channel your energy. Don't try to completely eliminate it.

DAM POWER

Have you visited a dam? Our family visited the Grand Coulee Dam in Washington State when I was a kid. As kids, our parents never cussed and we followed their example, but that day we came close. "Dad, look at those dam trees, next to the dam lake, on the other side of the dam road." Ridiculous but fun. I digress. Let's get back to helping you overcome nervousness by channeling the energy.

Thinking about dams will help you.

The Grand Coulee Dam extends 550 feet high and 500 feet wide. 5,185,400 acre·ft (6 km^3)-9,562,000 acre·ft (12 km^3) of water is held behind a dam! This forms a massive reservoir (or artificial lake) where before a river ran through.

As the water is channeled into the penstocks of the dam, the force of the water moves the blades of a huge turbine. This movement is captured into hydroelectric power-generating unit. The United States Bureau of Reclamation informs us that the Grand Coulee Dam produces "21 billion kilowatt-hours of electricity each year. That's enough power to supply 2.3 million households with electricity for one year." That is a lot of dam power.

As you get ready for your speech, a river of energy is building up in a reservoir. Nervousness, stress, chaotic care, fear, and anxiety are whelming up inside of you. Don't eliminate it. Don't become complacent or boring. Nor should you let it all out at once and become the speaker who spews words at the audience in an endless torrent of nervous energy.

Even dams have more than one way to release the power of the water. The penstocks can't handle all the weight of the power. The Hoover Dam is one of the most famous dams. Even this mighty wall of steel and concrete is not enough to contain the raw weight of water building up behind it. Water is not only channeled down the penstocks to provide useful electricity, multiple spillways are built into each dam so that water can be released without destroying the dam. The Hoover Dam can discharge 200,000 cubic feet per second at a velocity of 120 miles per hour! That is the same raw power of the Niagara Falls! That is a lot of dam power.

Don't eliminate the power building up in you.

Don't wait until the last minute to release it. You will become a Niagara Falls of information that will wash over everyone, leaving them with no idea of what just happened. That is what happened to me in that opening story when I stood in front of my college. A torrent of words were released. None were remembered.

When the day comes to give your speech, use these three "penstocks" to slowly release the nervousness and create positive energy in your speech.

PENSTOCK #1: USE PAUSES

Purposeful pauses are powerful. They create a void, which the audience fills with their attention. Audiences will lean in to hear what is on the other side of the…

… pause.

Pauses also allow you to take a deep breath. Pauses allow you to control the torrent of words. Pauses allow you to regain composure. Pauses allow you to be present.

Learn the power of the pause.

There are two words I write on my speech manuscripts repeatedly. "PAUSE" is one of them. When you purposefully pause, you take control of your nerves instead of allowing your nerves to control you. This makes you feel confident instead of rushed. This reminds you that you know what you are doing. This allows you to breathe deeply.

PAUSE.

PENSTOCK #2: SHOW PURPOSE.

Never pace the stage. Those who pace do so out of nervousness. It is distracting and obnoxious. Get your pacing out at the first practices. Then learn to knock it off. If you pace in practice, you will pace during your speech.

Instead of pacing, you should purposefully move. For a three-point speech, you should move to three areas in the form of triangle. Combined with the pause, this allows you gain composure and exert energy. Purposeful movements also punctuate your points.

How do you move with purpose? Video yourself. Yes, you will be embarrassed. Better to be embarrassed by yourself than in front of a group of people. Watch your movements. Take note of what to stop doing and what to add.

Purposeful movements during a speech provide a mental and physical outlet for your nervousness. Actors practice purposeful movement in theatre. Comedians pre-plan where they stand and how to use physical comedy. Stage magicians map out where to go and when. Learn from them.

PENSTOCK #3: LIGHT UP WITH PASSION.

John Wesley stirred up England in the 1700s. He was a passionate man who created incredible communities of faith throughout the land. He led a massive revival where hundreds of thousands of people rekindled their desire for a faith that had been dying. An already incredible thinker, writer, and author, John Wesley excelled in speaking. This quote is often attributed to him, even if it doesn't show up in any of his writings. I don't know its true origin, but I do know that it was true of John Wesley, and it can be true of you.

"Light yourself on fire with passion, and people will come from miles to watch you burn."

A passionate speaker is a captivating speaker. This is Martin Luther King Jr.'s speech, "I have a dream." This is JFK's, "Do not ask your country what it can do for you, but what you can do for your country." This is Billy Graham, Steve Jobs, Oprah Winfrey, John Maxwell, Bill and Melinda Gates, Anderson Cooper, Craig Groeschel, TD Jakes, Preacher Lawson, and any number of other speakers who grab your attention.

This can be you. You don't have to be a president, a CEO, a famous preacher, or a TV host. You just have to have the energy of care.

Care about the people you are speaking to.

Care about getting your point across to *them*.

Care about the content of your words. Yes, this can be a wedding toast, business proposal, presentation to your coworkers, interview, or detailed report to your boss. It doesn't matter what the content is as long as you make it matter to *you*.

Take that nervousness. Take your care. Take all your preparation, and let it burn through you.

You can do this. You will be amazing. People will want to hear you because you obviously care. They will be drawn to your passion for them and for the words you say.

ACTION:
SPILL YOUR EXTRA ENERGY

Here are three ways to practice channeling your extra energy.

1. Preparation.

2. Exercise.

3. Breathe.

ONE: PREPARATION.

Test day always made me nervous in high school, but it made my sister feel energized. The difference lay in the way we prepared. My sister studiously examined all her notes for weeks and months. She completed every assignment. She read every page.

I did not. I paid attention in school, did what I had to, hung out with friends, and then panicked the day of the test.

Both of us had energy coursing through our body when test day came. Both of us carried stress. Why was she more positive? Because she was prepared. She channeled her stress into daylong study sessions, test prep, and study groups. When the test came, she still had nervousness and stress, but she was able to direct it the way she had prepared.

And me? I emptied all my nervous energy onto the test page and produced the longest answers to each question. I let all my pent-up information out and vomited words using my pen.

The more energy you use to prepare before the event, the less negative energy you will have during the event. Your prior planning will prevent poor performance.

Channel your energy into preparation. Write out your speech. Turn it into note cards. Practice in front of the mirror. Practice to anyone who will listen. Practice to a coach. Let the coach critique you. Rewrite the speech. Put it on new note cards. Practice in front of the mirror. Practice to your friends. Practice in your car.

The first time you give the speech should never be the first time you say the speech.

Practice, practice, and practice. Practice to anyone who will listen. The more you practice, the more prepared you will be.

"Mike, that sounds like a lot of effort!"

Effort is energy at work. As you direct energy towards your preparation through practice, you will have less energy distracting you in your presentation.

> ### #ProTip:
>
> • Attend speech workshops such as ToastMasters and the Dale Carnegie Institute.
>
> • Hire a coach to give you feedback.
>
> • Invite friends to listen to you.
>
> • If you go to church, do a small group where you can share in front of others.
>
> • Join your Chamber of Commerce or networking events.

TWO: EXERCISE.

Lou taught me how to punch. I remember hitting those heavy bags as my mind replayed the problems I faced at work. I transformed stress into motion. I hit the bags harder and stayed in the gym longer as my coach moved me from exercise to exercise. Often, I went to the gym tense and left relaxed.

Hit the gym. Take a run. Go for a walk. Get your blood pumping and the energy flowing. If you use lots of your energy for physical exertion, you will have less energy for emotional exhaustion.

#ProTip:

If you are really worried about your upcoming speech, then follow this workout format (doing whatever type and amount of exercise fits you.)

5 days away:	Do some exercise.
4 days away:	Normal day.
3 days away:	Light workout. Eat healthy.
2 days away:	Go big! Do it. Exhaust yourself. Eat healthy.
1 day away:	Rest. Eat healthy.
Day of:	

Do a light workout. Focus on stretching. Eat healthy. Make *sure* you eat. Don't skip. You can eat light, but still eat.

THREE: BREATHE.

Most people fail to breathe enough. There are books and blogs on why deep breathing is important. There are other books and blogs on how to breathe. Ultimately, deep breathing works.

Taking time to breathe deeply restores you at a cellular level. It calms you from the core of your being. Deep breathing is correlated with peacefulness, stillness, and calm. Conversely, short breaths are characteristic of panic attacks. Turn your panic into peace by learning to breathe deeply.

Practice breathing deeply several days before your event so that you are ready to perform deep breaths the day of your event.

Here is a basic exercise I practice (note: I am not a trained health expert.)

1. Sit in a comfortable position.

2. Place one hand on my chest and another on my stomach.

3. Close my eyes.

4. Breathe in through my nose.

5. Be mindful that my belly pushes my hand out (chest remains still.)

6. Breathe out through open lips.

7. Take note of my belly going in.

8. Repeat 6 more times.

9. Be aware of my body and breathe.

10. Open my eyes and smile.

Practice these three spillways to be ready for your speech.

1. Prepare.

2. Exercise.

3. Breathe.

"So do not worry about tomorrow;
for tomorrow will care for itself."

Christ Jesus

STRATEGY #7:
BE IN THE MOMENT

The day arrived. Taylor and I were finally getting married. The ceremony began. The officiant walked me out onto stage. Our wedding party began to slowly approach the stage. Each groomsman accompanied a bridesmaid. The flower girls littered the floor with petals. Music changed. This was the moment. Everyone stood. Taylor's father began to walk her down the aisle. Time froze.

Everything was perfect.

Perhaps you have experienced the euphoria I'm talking about.

As I recall that moment, I get goosebumps. It is a moment worth reliving. It seemed as though time stood still while Taylor and I pronounced our love. However, not everything was perfect. Earlier we had a music mishap and the playlist we poured energy into creating went unused. We spent hours setting up candles only to find out that, because of the new carpet in the venue, we couldn't use real candles. There was some friendship and family drama we had to address. Our photographer didn't do as we asked. The hairstylist missed the mark. And further craziness I do not wish to relive. Not everything was perfect, but when Taylor walked down the aisle, none of the imperfection mattered. Only that moment mattered.

This is the moment that matters. Even as you read this, take a pause. This moment matters. You are here now. Be *here*, right now.

THE IRONY OF AGES AND STAGES

When I was 5, I wanted to be 10. When I was 10, I wanted to be 15. When I was 15, I wanted to be 16. When I was 16, I wanted to be 18. When I was 18, I wanted to be 21. When I was 21, I wanted to be 25.

When I was 30, I wanted to be 25. Now that I'm almost 40, I want to be 21.

Can you relate? When you were younger, you wanted to be older. Now that you are older, you want to be younger. The irony! We often want to be a different age than we are.

In life, we get so busy wanting to be somewhere else that we forget to be where we are.

My guess is that right now, you want to be on the other side of having delivered your speech. You just want to "get this over with". There are three stages of learning in a speech. If you keep thinking of skipping to *there*, then you won't learn *here*.

First Stage of Learning:
PREPARATION.

In speech preparation, you will research content and develop speaking skills. That is exciting! Don't wish it to be over, or you will miss out on what you can learn now. Don't be the 15-year-old that desperately wants to be an adult. You will miss out!

DEVELOP SKILLS: Learn how to present. Learn fluency. Increase your vocabulary. Understand the power of presence. Practice cadence, pace, and pauses. This is exciting. Learn some new skills that will help you in your speech and beyond!

Being present in preparation will grow a much larger skillset.

CONTENT: Depending on the type of your speech, this will be an exciting time to explore new areas of your expertise, or it will be a time to learn brand new information.

Being present in preparation will grant you more knowledge and deeper understanding. Don't miss it. Be present.

Second Stage of Learning:
PRESENTATION

In the presentation stage of learning, you learn to hone your people skills. This is no longer about content; it is about connection. By the time you arrive at the presentation, you must put aside your concerns about what you are saying and work on connecting with your audience. This means that you might lose some of the content. That is okay. Remember this:

What you lose in content, you gain in connection.

The presentation stage is where you learn about what your audience wants and needs. Don't miss out. Don't wish you could go back to rewrite your words. Don't rush through to the finish. Stay in the moment. Notice what people react to. Watch what makes them nod. Use your energy to energize them.

In one-on-one conversations, we can tell when someone is not listening. We can tell if someone checks out of the conversation in these personal settings. Likewise, we can tell if a communicator is "in his head". If you are not fully present when you speak, then you will miss out on what you can learn from your audience. And they will miss out on you.

Don't run back to what you "should have" written. Don't tie yourself to your notes. Don't rush ahead. Be there with the audience. Make it about them.

THIRD STAGE OF LEARNING:
REFLECTION

Often, we complete a task, only to immediately move onto the next. This fails to allow us to relish our victories or learn from our failures. This happens in public speaking as well. Reluctant speakers often express, "Wow, I'm so glad to be done with that!" without realizing that taking a moment of reflection will grant insights into both the content communicated and the connection created with the audience.

Take time (even 5 minutes) to do a quick Celebrate—Cut—Change (CCC) of your speech. It doesn't matter if it is a simple work presentation, a school speech, a wedding toast, or a high-level engagement. Take time to CCC.

CELEBRATE.

What did you do well? What worked? Know it so that you can repeat it.

CUT.

What did not work out well? What do you need to avoid? Note it, so that you don't repeat it.

CHANGE.

What could be better? What can you edit? Mark it so that you can improve it next time.

Stand-up comedians have their own way of doing this process. They will create content and then present it at a small club. There, they see which parts of their content allow them to create connections with the group. They celebrate and keep the good. They cut the bad. They change, tweak, and improve the weak jokes. As a result, a stand-up comedian continually improves.

Take a note from the professional stand-up comedian: learn in the preparation, learn in the presentation, and learn through the reflection. This improves you and increases your effectiveness in the future.

Don't skip ahead. Take a moment to enjoy not only your age, but also the stage of your public speaking journey.

WE LIVE IN AN INSTAGRAM WORLD

How often do you check social media?

If you have been like me, then the answer can be: all the time. So, I deactivated my Facebook account for a while. Initially, I missed Facebook: the inspirational quotes, argumentative people, political debates, memes, videos of kids, and knowing what everyone else was doing. Then I experienced an epiphany. I had been too busy living vicariously through the lives of others to enjoy my present moment.

I'm on a mission to enjoy right now.

What do these have in common? Instagram. Snapchat. Twitter. Facebook. LinkedIn. Myspace... each platform can steal you away from living your life to wanting the life of another. These platforms can seduce us into a virtual existence where we fail to live in our own reality. These platforms *can* do that *if* we allow them to.

If you are not careful, you can begin to build the perfect Insta picture while loathing the person behind the filter.

If you are not careful, you will mentally compete with your own expectations and with the false avatars of real people.

If you are not careful, you will compare your work, performance, speaking, and success with the inflated and manicured lives of others.

You don't know them. You can't be them. You can't go back. You can't go forward. When it comes to your life, your skills and your speaking, put aside the social media mentality. Give it up. Here's why. Circle this. Write it on your mirror. Memorize this.

If you compare and compete, you will live in defeat.

Don't weigh yourself down with the burden of being someone else.

Your past is in the past. Your future is not determined. Don't weigh yourself down wondering what will happen and how will you do in "that" moment. Enjoy *this* moment.

#ENJOYRIGHTNOW

Be on a mission to enjoy right now.

Right *now*, you are working to overcome your fear of public speaking. Good work. I'm proud of you. You can do this. You really can! I know it because I did it. I know it because I see my clients do it. Right now, speaking with no fear is your priority.

Work it.

Really.

Use the understanding I provide here to change your perspective. Change the way you think about speaking, and you will change the way you speak. Dive in and do the exercises in this book. Change your perspective. Stand in the face of adversity and summon the courage to conquer your fear! You've got this.

Do the work. Enjoy the process. Be HERE now.

Then when the moment comes, this is what you do...

TODAY, YOU ARE GIVING THE SPEECH!

Relax. Are you ready? At this point, it doesn't matter.

Did you do all the exercises? Maybe, who cares? You can't change that.

Do you know your speech? You have notes. You know as much as you know. Smile.

Will others do better? Maybe. Probably. Forget about them. You be you.

Are people going to enjoy your presentation? Hopefully. Do your best. Leave the rest.

Can you help the audience? Yes. You are here for this group. Speak to them.

Is failure possible? Not right now. Don't worry about later. You can't change it.

Should you have changed your speech? No should've or would've or could've. Drop it.

What could you do differently right now? Nothing. So be here.

The past cannot be changed.

The future is not determined.

This is now.

This moment is called your present.

Receive it like the gift that it is.

Enjoy the moment when you are getting ready for the speech. Enjoy overcoming the stress. Enjoy your practice. Live it. Embrace it. Be there.

When you give the speech: Channel the energy. Speak to one, not all. Breathe. Smile. Be you. Do your best. Be there.

What about after the speech?

WHATEVER HAPPENED, HAPPENED

Don't beat yourself up. Don't applaud yourself too hard. Smile. Whatever happened, happened. Accept it. No matter what, don't regret it. You did what you did. Smile. Keep your head up. Be proud that you faced your fear. You are a rockstar! Now, it doesn't matter how awesome you did. It doesn't matter if you think you did poorly. All that matters is how you can get even better.

Here's what you do after the event. Post event checklist:

- IMMEDIATELY AFTER.

  Smile. You did it. Just enjoy the moment.

- THE DAY OF:

  DO NOT focus on ANYTHING negative. Don't fish for compliments. Smile at yourself. Be proud of yourself. Applaud yourself. Enjoy the sensation of completion.

- THE DAY AFTER:

Relive the moment so that you can learn from it. Approach this as an interested third party. If you can watch your speech, then do that. Write down 3 things you can do better next time. 3 things, not 30. It's very hard to work on 30 different areas of improvement. However, you can improve 3 areas. Don't be overly critical. Build yourself up, don't tear yourself down.

This is very important. One HUGE key to getting better is debriefing on how you did. Do this the day after. You may invite someone to help you as well.

- THE DAYS AFTER:

Smile. Enjoy the memory of *that* moment.

If you did great with the speech, well done. Don't get seduced by your success. Enjoy the memory of the past moment. Know that you did well in the past moment, but live in the present moment.

If you did very poorly, it's okay. Don't get defeated by your supposed failure. You are a success in the simple fact that you did it! Roll your shoulders back, take a deep breath, and smile.

If you can't shake feeling bad about your speaking, then go back to Strategy #1: Uncover and Clean the Wound. Ask yourself, why did I allow this speech to have this effect on me?

LAST-MINUTE ADJUSTMENTS

Rarely do I suggest that beginning speakers make changes the day of the speech. The bigger the speech, the more prep it has taken. More preparation means that the speaker is settled into a groove. Don't try to change your groove the day of.

There are three simple adjustments I recommend the day of the speech. You can make these in the moment.

1. Gently roll your shoulders back.

2. Take a deep breath.

3. Don't forget to smile.

"Mike, you've already told me to breathe and smile." Yes, and I will say it again. Here is a simple reason why this is a good last-minute adjustment:

When you change your posture, breathing, and expressions, you change how you feel.

Don't change your outline, your points, your structure, or your presence. Simply make some minor adjustments. Roll back your shoulders. Take a deep breathe. Smile.

SOME FINAL WORDS FROM A WISE MAN

Ancient Jewish literature tells the story of the wisest king ever, King Solomon. Solomon was a marvel. He built upon the success of his father. He developed the small nation of Israel to be the world's superpower. For forty years, he ruled this small nation. In that time, silver became as common as stones. Vast structures were built in ways we don't even understand (he moved massive stones from a distant quarry to the top of Jerusalem to create the Temple). The world sought out his wisdom. The world today still benefits from thousands of his proverbs, poems, stories, and songs.

Near the end of his life, he wrote *Ecclesiastes*, a book exploring the meaning of life. He tells his own story of how he built an empire and chose to use his wealth, fame, education, and experience to see what would bring happiness to his heart. He did it all. He had around 1000 relationships with women. He amassed a fortune worth billions. He accumulated luxuries beyond what we can experience today. He was revered by the world. He led a full life by every standard. What did he conclude?

"So I commend the enjoyment of life, because there is nothing better for a person under the sun than to eat and drink and be glad. Then, joy will accompany them in their toil all the days of the life God has given them under the sun."—King Solomon (in Ecclesiastes 8:15, NIV translation)

Solomon's final words? Enjoy right now. This is true for life. It is true for all areas of life, including your speech.

Be in the moment. Not ahead. Not behind. Be right there.

MY "WHATEVER HAPPENED, HAPPENED" MENTALITY

For years I've run events. Before the event, we work like crazy to get ready. We push and stress and correct and plan. I'm meticulous and thorough. At times, I've annoyed my team as we got ready to execute the event.

Inevitably, every event has something go awry. My team looks at me nervously when this happens. They expect me to get angry, annoyed, irritated, critical, or confrontational. But I don't (usually).

My teams have expressed surprise that mishaps don't bother me in the moment. They presume, "He was stressed and high-strung before the event. This is going to push him over!" But it doesn't.

Why do I stress and worry and plan and prepare and nitpick and push before the event?

Because I can do something about it.

Why do I smile, shrug, and say, "It will be okay," when problems occur?

Because I can't change what happened.

Use your stress to push you to prepare before the event. Channel the anxiety of your upcoming speech into getting ready for the speech. Do the exercises. Take action. Work hard. Prior planning prevents poor performance. Go. Go! GO! You can get better. You can do this. You've got this! Get ready for that event!

Everything you do to get ready matters! Hire a coach. Rewrite the speech before the event.

Do *everything* you can!

...

...

...

...

...

Then...

When the event happens...

When you have to speak...

Just be there.

Could you have done more to be ready? Maybe.

It doesn't matter now. Just smile.

When the event happens and you have to speak, enjoy the moment.

Whatever prep has gone into writing the speech has passed. This is not the time to stress. This is the time to deliver.

You will be fine.

As you get ready for the speech, say to yourself:

"I will be fine. I will do my best. I am here, and I am going to enjoy this moment."

ACTION:
ENJOY RIGHT NOW.

Now is the time to train your mind to think of now. Learn to live beyond regrets and without worries. If you learn the art of enjoying right now, then you will be in the moment when the speech comes.

3 ways to train your mind to think of now:

1. Take in the details.

2. Create a gratitude list.

3. Live it and enjoy it.

ONE: TAKE IN THE DETAILS

My wife and I watch *The Punisher* on Netflix. The villain, Jigsaw, commonly flies into a rage as he tries to piece together what happened to him. He keeps revisiting the past and he can't control his violent emotions. When this happens, the psychiatrist routinely advises, "Name five blue details in the room". This act of taking in the details calms him and he reenters the moment.

This TV trick works in real life. It doesn't just stem from an actress on TV; real psychiatrists teach this technique for road rage, anger, and anxiety. It works.

It will work for you. It will slow you down. It will bring you back to the moment. Here is my non-psychiatric advice for you. Begin training yourself to live in the moment now. When the speech comes, you can be in *that* moment. You will be ready to deliver your talk instead of focusing on what you could have done or what might happen. Learn to live now.

If you learn to notice what is around you, you will also learn to notice the people with their needs and wants when you speak. So go ahead. Pause from reading or listening to this book. What are five blue details around you right now?

TWO: CREATE A GRATITUDE LIST

Every morning and every night, I take note of three things for which I'm grateful. This has helped me be present instead of being preoccupied with what happened or with what might happen.

In 2018, I stumbled upon *The How of Happiness* by Sonja Lyubomirsky. This renowned professor and psychologist received degrees from Stanford and Harvard. After extensive research, she recommends some simple strategies to increase happiness and decrease stress. One of them? Create a gratitude list.

Regularly working on a gratitude list has proven to reduce worry and anxiety.

Before you speak, take note of three specific things you appreciate. "I'm almost done" can't be one of them. Instead simply stop and reflect on what you appreciate in your life. Let the worry fade away as you focus on what you appreciate. Smile as you think through the specifics of what you are grateful for.

Gratitude works to reduce worry and anxiety in life, and it will work for your speech.

THREE: LIVE IT AND ENJOY IT

One of our modern-day poets gave this wise advice:

> Look
> If you had
> One shot
> Or one opportunity
> To seize everything you ever wanted
> In one moment
> Would you capture it
> Or just let it slip?

> You better lose yourself in the music, the moment
> You own it, you better never let it go
> You only get one shot, do not miss your chance to blow
> This opportunity comes once in a lifetime

> You can do anything you set your mind to...

> Lose Yourself lyrics © Kobalt Music Publishing Ltd. as performed by Eminem.

The moment you used to dread is coming ("used to" because you are now facing your fear). When it comes, live it. You only have it once.

Lean in. Be present. Act on the strategies. Discard your worries. Speak to one. Remember that it is not about you. You can do this. I believe in you.

Two last words:

Breathe. Smile.

"I think I can. I think I can. I think I can."

The Little Engine That Could

CONCLUSION

Twice I've tried CrossFit. The first time, I hit it hard. I was in there four or five times per week putting in a full workout. I gave it my all. Soon after I joined, people remarked on the development of my shoulders. I worked hard and it showed.

Then, my wife and I moved to California. Work picked up, and I tried to join CrossFit again, but I created excuses for why I couldn't show up all the time. I improved a bit, but not enough to get noticed. I didn't work hard, and it showed.

In the second scenario I could blame the GYM, but the reality was simply that I didn't do the work.

The more you put in, the more you will get out.

Throughout my years of coaching people, there is one constant: our returns are determined by our investment. Choose to invest in yourself. How?

START HERE: 1-2-3-R

1. BELIEVE.

Believing in yourself is the foundation on which to implement these 7 Strategies. Fill your mind with positive affirmations and begin to change the way you think.

2. PUT IT ON YOUR CALENDAR.

Pull out your phone or your planner and map out one hour to work on one strategy. You must put it on your calendar. If you are skimming this, or reading on vacation, or listening to the audiobook, then pause for a moment. Take this action. Schedule a time slot this week for you to begin to work on a strategy. Don't push it off too far.

Once you schedule that one hour, make sure you show up to this important meeting with yourself. Then make sure to schedule your next one as well. For best results, schedule one hour every day for five days. After all, it's just like the gym: the more you put in, the more you will get out.

If you have one hour now, then go for it. Move on to step 3!

3. CHOOSE ONE STRATEGY.

Which strategy resonated with you the most? Which one do you need to get to work on?

1. Uncover & Clean the Wound

2. Imagine the Worst

3. You Be You

4. Speak to One

5. It's Not About You

6. Channel The Power

7. Be in the Moment

Choose one strategy to work on for one hour. Look up your selected strategy and start to read it again. You will see that there are three aspects woven throughout this book: perspective, preparation, and practice.

These three components should be braided together. These three provide a full body workout. Changing your perspective is like strengthening your core and willpower. Preparing yourself is like strengthening your base. That is like putting in a good leg day at the gym. Practicing will lead people to see noticeable results. This is that upper body strength that men want to wow women with.

Don't be the girl who just works one area. Don't be the guy who skips leg day. Weave these together for a strong workout. All three areas are key:

A. Change your perspective.

B. Invest in preparation.

C. Take time to practice.

Use these ABC's as you work on your strategy. For example, if you need to learn to Channel the Power, then:

A—Change your perspective by understanding your energy flow as discussed in the chapter.

B—Invest in preparation by looking for groups to practice with or by hiring a coach. Prepare yourself for your speech by practicing cadence, paces, and pauses.

C—Practice the principle of energy transference. Do this by working out or by strategically using your motions and movements as you practice your speech.

R—Repeat until complete.

MAKE IT YOURS

1. Believe.

2. Put it on your calendar.

3. Choose a strategy.

    a. Change your perspective.

    b. Invest in preparation.

    c. Take time to practice.

R. Repeat until complete.

ONE LAST ENCOURAGEMENT

You *can* do this.

I did this. I was able to overcome my fear.

Others have done this. I've worked with people just like you. Fear no longer controls them.

Simply start doing what you need to do to get where you want to be. Maybe you won't erase your fear in one day or one week or one month, but you will ease your fear. You will learn to channel that nervousness into an engaging presence. You *will* do great. You really will.

You can do this.

You don't have to live in fear any longer.

DISCOUNT FOR A COACHING SESSION

Do you want to sign up for a coaching session? Receive a $60 discount when you go to: http://discount.stepstoadvance.com/book

Working together with clients, I get to see dedicated people make incredible advances. If you want more coaching and more guidance, I would love to help you build on the success you are beginning to see through this book.

Visit my site at http://discount.stepstoadvance.com/book to sign up to receive a $60 discount as you schedule a one-on-one coaching session to help you take your next step.

ABOUT MIKE ACKER

Mike Acker is a leadership and communications coach, author, and pastor with over 18 years of experience in speaking, leadership development, and organizational management.

Known for his authenticity, humor, and engaging presence, Mike specializes in fomenting personal and organizational awareness, allowing clients to create their own personal growth track. His approach is earnest, informed, and holistic, leading to a more satisfying balance in work and life. His expertise in communications and leadership has attracted politicians, business entrepreneurs, educational leaders, and executive managers.

Mike's training stretches from private Spanish speaking schools in Mexico, national college debate tournaments, master classes in cultural leadership, certifications in coaching, and his current MBA. Mike has been a professional speaker for 18 years and has spoken to groups of 10 to 10,000.

In 2014, Mike accepted the role of Chairman of the Board for an international non-profit, which works to lift kids out of poverty in Senegal and Mexico. In this capacity he works with the paid staff, the board of directors, and the international staff as they collaborate to sponsor families, start schools, and build dozens of feeding centers. (https://www.goonthemission.com)

Mike also enjoys rock-climbing, wake surfing, skiing, church, building Legos with his son, and going on dates with his wife, Taylor. Mike believes in the power of prayer, exercise, journaling, and real community to counter the stresses of everyday life.

http://www.stepstoadvance.com

PAXTON WANTS TO KNOW IF YOU CAN HELP!

Can you help? If you liked this book and found it helpful, could you please take a brief moment to review it on Amazon?

Simply visit http://www.amazon.com/author/mikeacker to select *Speak with no Fear*. Then leave your honest feedback!

Reviews are extremely important to the success of a book! So if you like what you've read (or even if you didn't), then please take 2 minutes to help me out with a review. THANK YOU. I appreciate your feedback!

As a big THANK YOU for your review, e-mail contact@stepstoadvance.com with a link to your VERIFIED review, and you will get a free 30-minute coaching session with me. There, you can ask me any questions you have about speaking or career advancement!

DO YOU WANT MORE?

You are awesome! Thanks for asking.

I always have something new I'm working on. Sign up for my *New Releases* mailing list to get access to new articles, programs, discounts, freebies, and upcoming books!

TO GET STARTED, GO TO:
https://subscribe.stepstoadvance.com/me

Made in the USA
Columbia, SC
09 March 2020

88931221R00104